D1082200

# Loving: A Psychological Approach

# LOVING

# A Psychological Approach

Gardner Webb College Library

## HOWARD L. MILLER
*University of Alabama*

## PAUL S. SIEGEL
*University of Alabama*

**JOHN WILEY AND SONS**
New York • Chichester • Brisbane • Toronto

*Copyright* © *1972, by John Wiley & Sons, Inc.*

All rights reserved. Published simultaneously in Canada.

Reproduction or translation of any part of this work beyond that permitted by Sections 107 or 108 of the 1976 United States Copyright Act without the permission of the copyright owner is unlawful. Requests for permission or further information should be addressed to the Permissions Department, John Wiley & Sons, Inc.

*Library of Congress Cataloging in Publication Data:*

Miller, Howard Lee, 1937-
  Loving: a psychological approach

  Bibliography: p.
  1. Love. I. Siegel, Paul S., 1918-   joint author. II. Title.

BF575.L8M47                 155.3                 72-3770
ISBN 0-471-60390-2

Printed in the United States of America

10 9 8 7 6

This book is dedicated to:
our parents who taught us

love

and to:
Margaret and Helen
who bear the brunt of it.

# PREFACE

Today, perhaps more than ever before, all areas of human knowledge are being examined for their relevance to the real world and its current issues. The word "relevance" itself has come to sound trite; yet the challenge it implies has barely begun to be answered. Education, in particular, is being mercilessly scrutinized for its value in solving the problems of society and of individuals. We believe this emphasis is long overdue. If we have learned in any way to cope with our personal problems and with our environment, it is clearly our duty as scientists and educators to refine and communicate this knowledge and application.

If today's education cannot meet the test of relevance for a major segment of our society, it must be modified or discarded. Psychology, in particular, must address itself to, and be applicable to, the needs of people. If our research and theorizing have developed any viable principles, let us apply them. This book represents such an effort. It will cure neither pollution nor poverty but maybe this attempted application of psychological knowledge to a concept that concerns most people will add some small increment to the enjoyment of life. Anyway, we hope so.

*Howard L. Miller*
*Paul S. Siegel*

# CONTENTS

# CHAPTER I

# Introduction

This is a book about love. Books about love are not rare. The claim to singularity of this particular book is that it presents love and its phenomena within a framework generated by well-established psychological theory. While conceding that it is indeed difficult to define love and to observe its effect with scientific rigor, we believe that some start can in fact be made toward a scientific analysis. Moreover, we feel that such an analysis can be made without detracting from the wonder and beauty of the phenomena of love. Understanding may prove to be a greater basis for appreciation than ineffability; we are proceeding in any case, under that assumption.

Certainly, few people would contest the statement that love is a viable concept in our society and affects us, if for no other reason, because many of us believe in it. But simple belief is not definition; and definition has proved evasive. In spite of this, love, even ill defined, has displayed some remarkable attributes. In a study of 158 well-adjusted children, Langdon and Stout (1951) concluded that the fact that the children were well loved was not only the most important factor apparently related to their adjustment but it was also the only factor common to all of them. The concept of love, then, would seem to be an important one in our lives.

We assume, here, that love is not only a viable concept but also an observable phenomenon and susceptible to analysis. The framework we shall use for this analysis is familiar in psychology and has commanded much attention within the field in general, but has had surprisingly little application to love. We are speaking of the theory and study of learning.

Although our posture in this book is largely theoretical, we hope that a major virtue will prove to be practical applicability. While not

1

principally a how-to-do-it type manual, we shall, in fact, devote much space to the essential questions of living with love. Immediate usefulness is, thus, a prime goal, the realization of which must ultimately be judged by each individual reader. Along these lines, we must add that the primary topic of this book is love and not sex; but it is neither desirable nor even possible to ignore the central role of sex in some types of love. We shall insist that sex and love are indeed separable but also synergistic in combination. Sex gets its full due in the development of erotic love. Perhaps more important, practical aspects of the role of sex in life and love will be considered and suggestions for the enhancement of life, love, and sex will be proposed.

At this point it might be helpful to try to describe with greater precision just what phenomena we shall be dealing with. We talk about many different kinds of love, or at least we use the word in many different ways. Are these truly different phenomena? Or, are they all the same except for differences in "direction"? Mustn't there be some common feeling found in all situations wherein we say we love something? People talk about love of pets, love of friends, parents, children, husbands, wives, mistresses, lovers, abstract principles, and even inanimate objects. Surely these widely different things cannot all inspire exactly the same feelings and responses! We shall concede these very real differences and explore them in detail later, but first we shall turn to an examination of whatever element (or elements) all of these feelings share in common that cause us to at least use the same word to describe them.

The most obvious commonality is that we value all of these things. We wish, in some way, to possess them, be with them, and protect them even if, at the moment, they are not useful to us in any practical way. We wish to live in a country that we love, spend time with people we love, keep and protect our loved pets, and so on. Significantly though, this desire does not depend on any special need or mood. We don't wish to be with people we love only when they are serving our whims; our feelings for loved objects are much more general than that. To put it in other words, we have a tendency (or wish) to approach the loved object and this tendency is not wholly dependent on any particular need (or drive). Our desire for the object, then, is not specific to any single situation, but cuts across many different ones. A hamburger may look very good to us when we are hungry, but normally we would exhibit a marked indifference to it when we are sated. Even our most tempting and favorite foods would not attract us particularly when we are full. We cannot, therefore, love food. Similarly, it is easily imaginable that there may be many people whom we do not love but may wish to have sexual contact with when we are in the mood. We might be rather indifferent to these people at other times. Although we would normally have even stronger erotic feelings for people with whom we are in love, the main difference between the two relationships is that we also value the latter individual and his company even when we are not sexually aroused.

Turning to other situations in which we can reasonably apply the word love, it seems that the same principles hold true. If we feel brotherly love for a family member or a friend, we enjoy being with him whether or not he is doing anything in particular for us at that moment. We are careful of his feelings, and we would generally take pains to protect him. Once again, these feelings are present across many different situations and are not wholly dependent on some particular state, need, or mood. When we say that we love a house (assuming, for now, that this is a meaningful statement), are we not saying that we enjoy occupying that particular house more than other houses that would serve our basic needs as well? Do we not mean that we enjoy that structure even when we don't require its shelter from the weather?

Immediately, many questions present themselves. When most people think about love, they think about love for other human beings, especially the opposite sex. And indeed, that will be our principal concern here. But what is this feeling? Is it the storied and wondrous top of the clouds thrill, the compelling conviction that this one particular human being is the most important one in the world? Is it the exciting physical sensation associated with being near or touching the loved person? Is there such a thing as love at first sight? What is infatuation and what relationship, if any, does it have to love? What is so-called "Platonic love," and what is sexual love? How are these similar, and how do they differ? And so on. The reader will undoubtedly entertain many questions of his own. Perhaps the most important of these will focus on how we can recognize and enjoy love more and how we can learn to love more satisfactorily and be loved more completely. It is intended and hoped that this book will answer these questions and others.

We are not yet ready for a formal definition of love. We are not even ready for a definitive description of situations in which it can meaningfully be said to exist. The question of what kinds of things can engender love will be addressed later. As a necessary but temporary expedient, however, let us begin with the suggestion that love is a broad and relatively stable enjoyment of interaction with the loved object, although it does not serve exclusively to satisfy one specific need. Does this statement describe reasonable behavior? Does it resemble any other human behavior; or is it perhaps some special and singular phenomenon that cannot be related to current explanations of other human actions? We believe that it is not only reasonable but that it can also be related to an existing broad conceptual framework. The fit is surprisingly good. Let us take a brief look into some of the characteristics of love behavior.

We are not born loving any particular person or object. Nor do we develop love for something in a vacuum of experience. To truly love anything we must have extensive interaction with it. We must learn how to love and what to love. It is in this way that loving is most readily analyzed as human behavior. Psychologists have spent a great deal of time studying how we learn. And they have learned quite a bit about learning. But does learning to love resemble other human learning? Can we really understand more about love by examining what we know about learning in general? Yes, we can. We learn what foods are tasty and when hungry, we turn to these. We learn what satisfies our thirst and where to find it. We learn what makes us warm when we are cold. What seems to be different about love is that there is no single and immediate state that determines exclusively when we should seek a love object. Moreover, we have well-accepted theories about why it is rewarding to eat a steak when we are hungry, why drinking water relieves our thirst, why it is rewarding to be warmed when we are cold, and so forth, but it is much harder to explain why it is rewarding simply to be in the presence of someone we love. It is by no means inexplicable; it is simply more difficult to understand fully in the context of our present psychological theories. There are more loose ends; and it is a more complex phenomenon. But before continuing with this general discussion, we introduce, in the next chapter, some of the language and theory of learning.

CHAPTER II

# Learning and Love

SUMMARY

In this book we have adopted the position that love is learned, in much the same fashion that anything else is learned. Chapter II provides the background in learning theory necessary to understand how this comes about. Of paramount importance is the concept of reinforcement; what is learned is controlled by reward and punishment, or by signals associated with reward and punishment.

Love is a form of approach behavior. The loved person is approached because of frequent but not entirely predictable association with many different kinds of rewarding experience.

Extinction (unlearning), spontaneous recovery (return of a response), generalization (transfer of training), and discrimination (telling a difference between two signals) all influence the strength of approach behavior. Concept formation and the self-concept also play a strong role.

Love is a learned response. And like hunger or thirst, it is motivating; associated with it is an impulse to do something; to act. By "learned" we mean that love is largely a product of experience; that it is not given by nature. For example, although the expression "learning to walk" is common, we actually mature to walk; it is an ability that nature gives us, and practice or training play little or no role. Not so with love. The biology of love we take to be entirely secondary to learning. By "response" we do not intend the dictionary meaning of the term. The love response is an emotion. It is an internal reaction. It is an expectancy. It is central or "in the mind." It is a feeling. It may involve the autonomic (automatic or involun-

5

tary) nervous system. It is all of these. It cannot be observed in any direct way by the public, but possesses a compelling private reality.

Closely associated with the love response is the impulse to act; to do something, and the action is one of approach to something or somebody. Approach must not be thought of exclusively as a physical movement of the body through space, that is, as an actual locomotion (although it may be). Approach is "psychological" movement. Thus, the young man whose eye follows the passing girls is "approaching." The yearning to be with another is equally an approach response, albeit an incipient one.

There are alternative accounts of just how anything gets learned. Psychologists are not in total accord on this. We shall employ a set of principles held in at least similar form by a substantial number of contemporary learning theorists. Our treatment is closely related to the position developed by O. H. Mowrer (1960).

## Fear, Hope, and Reinforcement

Higher forms of animal life (man in particular) come to respond emotionally to signals of impending events. These signs ("stimuli" to the psychologist) take on the emotional loading of the event they forecast. Those associated with punishing (aversive) events become fear signals; those associated with pleasure ("good feelings") become hope signals. Fear signals predict pain; hope signals predict reward or relief. To illustrate with an example from the animal laboratory of the psychologist: If we should repeatedly present a buzzer to a white rat in his home cage and follow it with an electric shock to his feet, he will soon learn to fear the buzzer. He cannot tell us about his fear (the internal response), of course, but we can readily infer it from what we can see and hear. After a few associations with shock, when the buzzer is sounded, he crouches and lays back his ears. Perhaps he defecates or urinates. He may squeal. In other words, he looks and sounds frightened. Significantly, these behaviors are quite different from his first response to the buzzer. Before its association with pain (when "neutral"), the buzzer produced little more than a momentary pause in his normal daily routine. We say that the animal has learned fear; through experience the buzzer has taken on a different "meaning." It now signals impending pain. It is threatening. It has become a fear-producing signal. And, if we provide the animal with the means to control the buzzer, to turn it off, he will do just that. If, for example, we so arrange it that when he steps on a little treadle, he can turn off the buzzer, he will come to do so whenever the buzzer is presented. To turn off the buzzer is to turn off the fear. This is clearly a two-step theory. First the animal learns to fear a signal and then he acts to do something about it. That is, he behaves in a way that will reduce his fear. Let's now label the major events in this learning situation.

The original cause of pain and fear, the shock, we shall call a *primary negative reinforcer* . . . that term will be applied from now on to any stimulus or event that is more or less naturally unpleasant, punishing, or aversive. Characteristically, all animals (man included, of course) move away from or act in such a way as to escape or minimize primary negative reinforcers. The buzzer, and all such signals that take on a fear or anxiety loading through association with a primary negative reinforcer, we shall call *secondary or learned negative reinforcers*. Alternatively, we shall refer to them as fear or danger signals. Significantly, the animal's response to a learned negative reinforcer is quite like his response to the primary negative reinforcer; he moves away from it. He makes effort to escape it. It is dangerous. It evokes fear. It predicts pain or discomfort.

Let's look next at the positive or rewarding side, the learning of hope. Again we choose to illustrate with an example from the animal laboratory. Another white rat is readily available. This time we present the buzzer but we follow it with food. The food drops into a little pan from which he has eaten in the past. He is hungry. He approaches the food and eats it. His hunger is reduced. He feels better. The food, like the shock, is a primary reinforcer, but unlike shock, it is *positive*. Rather than away from it, he moves toward it. The food both attracts and holds him. And we call this *approach behavior*. After several presentations of buzzer and food, the buzzer becomes a secondary or learned reinforcer, but this time it is positive. The rat will "move toward" the buzzer. Or, more accurately, he will act to bring the buzzer to him. If provided the means to do so, he will turn on the buzzer. It is a hope signal. It signals good things to come, just as in the case of the first rat, it signaled bad things to come (fear). If we present the same treadle to the second rat, rigged to turn on the buzzer, he too will soon step on it promptly. This behavior (treadle pressing) is also an approach response, but it is learned approach.

Secondary positive reinforcers or hope signals "promise" relief from tension, pain, or discomfort, and it actually makes little difference whether the source of discomfort is rooted in the biological makeup as is true of hunger, or results from a learned response to a secondary negative reinforcer (anxiety or fear in response to a danger signal). If the signal is followed by relief, by the reduction of discomfort regardless of source, it takes on the property of a secondary positive reinforcer or hope signal. It will evoke approach behavior in the future.

Let's now pause to summarize. Here is the important terminology presented so far.

*Primary Negative Reinforcer.* An event (or stimulus) that is more or less naturally punishing or aversive. Pain or discomfort is felt.

*Secondary or Learned Negative Reinforcer.* An event (signal or stimulus) that has become punishing or aversive through its association with a primary negative reinforcer. Fear or anxiety is experienced in its presence. We shall refer to this stimulus as a fear or danger signal.

*Escape Behavior or Escape Response.* Act of moving away from or reducing a negative reinforcer. This may be unlearned (response to a primary negative reinforcer) or learned (response to a secondary or learned negative reinforcer). Since escape from a secondary or learned negative reinforcer serves to prevent the occurrence of (avoids) actual punishment (primary negative reinforcer) it is usually called avoidance or an avoidance response.

*Primary Positive Reinforcer.* An event or stimulus that is more or less naturally rewarding. It is accompanied by relief or pleasant feelings. Food (when hungry) and water (when thirsty) are examples.

*Secondary or Learned Positive Reinforcer.* An event (stimulus or signal) that is rewarding because of its association with a positive reinforcer. In its presence, hope (promised relief) is felt. Stimuli can also become hope signals when associated with (predict) the relief of fear, a response to a secondary negative reinforcer.

*Approach Behavior or Approach Response.* Act of "moving toward," of maximizing or getting more of a positive reinforcer. It may be unlearned (response to a primary positive reinforcer) or learned (response to a secondary or learned positive reinforcer).

## Approach and Escape Behaviors

There are many ways to express escape and approach. Physical movement away from or toward stimuli or events is merely one way. This is usually the kind of behavior we require of a rat or a monkey in the animal lab to get him to tell us about his fears and hopes. We observe that he moves away from, or toward, some object. The human being, on the other hand, can express escape and approach in many other and much more subtle ways. He is vastly more versatile. We have mentioned the approach behavior of the young man who hangs on the corner, girl-watching. Pictures taken during World War II of German prisoners of war required to watch atrocity films taken in German concentration camps showed that most averted their eyes. They looked down or away from the screen. This is obviously escape behavior, as truly so as physically leaving the scene. This can be taken a step further. If a thought is unpleasant, threatening, or anxiety arousing, we escape by substituting another less threatening thought. So to speak, we change the subject. In more extreme instances, we escape such thoughts (fear or danger signals) by repressing them or "forgetting" them. These are the thoughts that are just too hot to handle. Approach can also be ideational or cognitive. Yearning for someone is a way of approaching that person. As we shall see later on, the escape and approach behaviors that go into the development of love are usually of this subtle kind.

Whether we identify a particular response as escape or as approach is usually a matter of where we wish to put the emphasis. In the final analysis, the distinction between the two usually collapses. Approach responses can be viewed (at least in part) as escape from some source of discomfort. And most escape responses take on an approach quality. In other words, to move toward something is to move away from something else, and vice versa. To escape the buzzer as a fear signal, the rat approaches and steps on the treadle. This reduces his fear. We shall make capital of this later.

Some of the attraction of the loved one (who, too, is a "stimulus" and will take on secondary reinforcing properties) results from this person's capacity to reduce anxiety. Just as the treadle is approached and "used" by the rat to escape fear, so the loved person may be approached and "used" to relieve anxiety. He can thus become a very powerful secondary or learned positive reinforcer or hope signal. The hope signal value (promised relief) of the loved one is, of course, influenced by many other social interactions as well, from back scratching to the reduction of erotic urges. More about this later.

## Extinction (Unlearning)

If primary reinforcement no longer follows the fear or hope signal, each gradually loses its capacity to evoke the emotion. This is known as "extinction." To illustrate, if we now present the buzzer repeatedly but no longer follow it with shock or with feeding, the buzzer's emotion arousing capability wanes. Fear and hope grow weaker as it becomes more and more certain that neither pain nor reward will follow. Thus, we speak of the extinction of fear and hope, and of the escape and approach responses based upon them. The latter will also extinguish in the absence of primary reinforcement. If never again shocked or fed, the rat will ultimately stop pressing the treadle even though the treadle continues to control the buzzer, turning it off or on as the case may be. This is scarcely surprising. The buzzer no longer arouses fear or hope. Its meaning is gone (or changed).

In extinction, an important difference between fear and hope signals is seen. Fears, and the escape behaviors based upon them, extinguish more slowly than hopes and associated approach behaviors. In other words, fear is a stronger or more pervasive emotion. One reason why escape behaviors resist extinction more strongly than approach is fairly obvious. Often the animal can escape a fear signal by actually leaving the scene. He runs away, in some sense. Thus, he cannot directly experience the failure of punishment to occur. And he continues to run away because his fear is reduced by doing so. On the other hand, the hope signal causes him to approach, putting him in a position to discover immediately that reward doesn't follow.

Just how long it takes for extinction to occur depends largely on how often, and when, a primary reinforcer is paired with the fear or hope signal during the learning phase. This is known as the *reinforcement schedule*, and a great deal of variation is possible, of course. If primary reinforcement always and invariably follows the signal during learning, with its discontinuation, extinction is usually rapid, at least far more so than if it had been scheduled occasionally but unpredictably. The occasional but unpredictable pairing of primary reinforcement with the signal is called a random intermittent reinforcement schedule and it is a reliable principle of learning that slow extinction (high resistance to extinction) follows.

Under some circumstances, after extinction has taken place, the animal may start once again to respond. Fear or hope, and associated escape and approach responses, may recover "spontaneously," that is, in the total absence of further primary reinforcement. Learning theorists call this "*spontaneous recovery.*" It is likely to occur after a change in the situation, or following some intervening activity, and it may occur more than once. Eventually, however, if reinforcement is never again presented, extinction will be complete, or nearly so. Almost as distressing to the therapist as to the patient, it is not uncommon to see in the clinical patient the spontaneous recovery of an old fear believed to have been fully extinguished.

## Generalization and Discrimination

Suppose that we now present to our fear-trained rat a slightly different sounding buzzer. Will this new signal also evoke fear? Will he continue to press the treadle to turn off the new signal? The answer, of course, is "Yes" to both questions. He generalizes. And the more closely the new signal resembles the old one, the more fully will he exhibit the same old behavior. This is called "*stimulus generalization.*" It is an important principle. If an animal did not respond in this way, he would soon perish, for, in his natural habitat, he rarely encounters exactly the same stimulus twice. Without generalization he would not benefit from "transfer of training." He would have to begin all over, so to speak. He would find himself in an always new learning situation.

Generalization is opposed by "*discrimination.*" If generalization is viewed as responding in the same way to somewhat different signals, discrimination implies responding in a different way to different signals. Thus, if the new buzzer is never reinforced, the rat will ultimately stop responding (stop generalizing). Extinction takes place. He will continue to respond to the old buzzer, of course, as long as we continue to reinforce with shock or food. At this point, the animal is exhibiting his capacity to tell the difference between the two stimuli. We say that he is discriminating. He behaves in a different way to the two signals.

*Concepts*

Generalization and discrimination play significant roles in the development of *concepts*. A concept is made up of several somewhat different stimuli that hang together as a group or class. And we respond in much the same way to all the stimuli making up that class, despite the fact that the stimuli differ in other ways. They share some common characteristic that makes it possible to classify them as alike (generalization). For example, there's the concept of "roundness." Ten balls may differ in many ways: some hard, some soft; some blue, some red; some large, some small, and so on. But each is at the same time alike, each is round. Each is capable of rolling. All ten might be used interchangeably and equally well in a game requiring a rolling object. Roundness is a fairly simple concept. Through judicious scheduling of reinforcement (and the action of generalization and discrimination), we could certainly teach it to a monkey. We could train him to respond in the same way to many different round objects (including some he has never seen before) while responding in a different way to other, say square, objects.

In his everyday living, the human being is constantly guided by concepts. From moment to moment, and from situation to situation, he responds in much the same way to stimuli that he has learned to classify as alike in some fashion. And many of these concepts are quite subtle, often complex and full of nuance. Each of us, for example, possesses a concept of "beauty" and "ugliness" as we see it in another person. A man will respond in some similar way to all women he perceives as "beautiful"; in a different way to those he perceives as "ugly." On the Stanford-Binet test of intelligence, the "normally" intelligent child of around four years of age will correctly identify as "pretty" or as "ugly" a pen sketch of a person's face. Successful performance is scored in terms of whether or not the child's label agrees with the cultural norm (what most people agree on as pretty or ugly). By the time we become adults, the concept of beauty in the opposite sex has become highly personal, and subjective—"is in the eye of the beholder"; and the personality of the other one has gotten all tangled up with his physical characteristics. His potential as a reinforcer has become paramount. Part of the old saying that "love is blind" is based on the fact that the perception of beauty in the opposite sex varies widely among different people.

The concept of beauty enters strongly into the love relationship; and so does "sex appeal," an obviously related concept. Sometimes we classify and respond to the physical characteristics of other people in terms of whether or not they lend themselves to bedroom fantasies; Raquel Welch, yes; Phyllis Diller, no. Interestingly enough, female white rats also vary widely in sex appeal. At least, in heat, some will attract many male rats; others, almost none.

It's time to pause and summarize again.

*Extinction.* Weakening and ultimate disappearance of a response with the failure of reinforcement. Just how quickly extinction takes place is determined largely by reinforcement history, how often, and when, reinforcement occurred during learning.

*Spontaneous Recovery.* The return of an extinguished response in the absence of further reinforcement.

*Generalization.* Transfer of a response from the signal or stimulus of original learning to a new and different stimulus. The more nearly the new stimulus resembles the old one, the more strongly will the response to the new stimulus resemble the response to the old stimulus.

*Discrimination.* Responding in a different way to two different stimuli; somewhat the opposite of generalization.

*Concept.* Group or class of stimuli that share some common, usually abstract, characteristic. We respond in much the same way to all stimuli making up the class. A form of generalization.

## The Self-concept

A concept of special significance is the self-concept or self-image, the picture of the self that each of us holds. This, too, is an abstraction like the "roundness" of a ball. Mostly, it is a kind of distillation of our past experiences of success and failure, our triumphs and defeats. It is a privately held picture of what we are and what we feel we can and cannot accomplish. Additionally, frequently causing us grief, the self-concept tells us what we should be.

We respond to the self-concept just as we respond to any other concept; in a consistent way. The self-image is personal and subjective. Rarely is it true that others ("outsiders") hold the same image of us. This theme is sensitively reflected in Edwin Arlington Robinson's poem, "Richard Cory."

The self-concept is the gauge against which we weigh all present successes and failures. Each of us evaluates personal accomplishment against the demands or goals of the self-concept. When we fail to measure up to these standards, we feel less worthwhile. This sense of personal worth is very much a part of the love relationship. Through reinforcement, lovers mutually enhance each other's self-concept. We turn to that story in the next chapter.

### Unpredictable Reinforcement

We have noted that a hope signal becomes more resistant to extinction when primary reinforcement follows intermittently (occasionally) but randomly (unpredictably). In other words, when the event that it signals is less than certain to follow, the secondary reinforcer takes on greater strength and a stronger capacity to evoke approach. This capability is further enhanced by varying the nature and the amount of primary reinforcement. If the buzzer is sometimes followed by food in varying amounts, sometimes by water in varying volumes, or sometimes a sex partner in varying degrees of sexual receptivity, for example, it can become a very powerful hope signal indeed. The key here is generality and the absence of certainty. The more kinds of primary reinforcement associated with the buzzer and the less predictable the reinforcement, the more resistant to extinction is the emotion of hope and the approach behavior that it causes. There are limits, of course. The schedule of primary reinforcement can become too "lean." Approach then becomes a kind of poor gamble. And extinction follows.

### Generalized Secondary Reinforcement

When associated with many rewarding events that differ in kind and amount, a secondary positive reinforcer is known as a *generalized* secondary positive reinforcer. It is a stimulus possessing an extensive history of association with many palpable rewards. It could just as well be called a generalized hope signal. Money and praise are ready examples. Each has been associated with the relief of many needs. And each is independent of any single or particular need. Each evokes strong approach behaviors. We are willing to work hard to obtain both.

At last we come to the pièce de résistance. *Love is a response to a generalized hope signal, a broad pleasurable expectancy. The love object, be it a "thing" or a person, is a generalized secondary positive reinforcer.* The loved object serves to attract and to hold. And it works across a broad spectrum of situations, circumstances, moods, and motivational states both learned and unlearned.

SUGGESTED READING

Any one of the following general psychology texts will introduce the reader to learning theory.

Kendler, H. H. *Basic psychology.* New York: Appleton-Century-Crofts, 1968. Chapters 7–9.

Kimble, G. A., & Garmezy, N. *Principles of general psychology.* New York: Ronald Press, 1968. Chapter 9.

Deese, J. *Principles of psychology.* Boston: Allyn and Bacon, 1964. Chapter 2.

Deese, J. & Hulse, S. W. *The psychology of learning,* 3rd edition. New York: McGraw-Hill, 1967. Also contains a relevant discussion of the learning issues raised, but at a level of complication and sophistication beyond that necessary to understand the principles used here. The student interested in pursuing learning theory to this extent might well consult this book.

# CHAPTER III

# Love's Early Course

SUMMARY

People can provide for each other many kinds of reinforcing or rewarding experiences; thus, they can become generalized secondary reinforcers or love objects. Early in life we develop fears about our worth and attractiveness to others. These feelings are difficult to extinguish and usually persist into adulthood. And so, when another person expresses interest in us, he becomes a powerful reinforcer, thus establishing the basis for the beginning of love. If our self-esteem is quite low, however, our ability to love will be handicapped.

An example of one way in which a love affair might develop is presented to illustrate these principles.

Honesty is essential to the quality of a continuing love relationship. Dishonesty chokes communication and introduces avoidance behaviors.

In Chapter I we acknowledged the existence of many different kinds of love. It was pointed out, however, that the one thing that all loved objects share is that pleasure in their presence is not dependent on a specific need state. Put another way, they are generally reinforcing. In Chapter II, it was shown that objects can become generally reinforcing when they are associated with different kinds of rewards, particularly if these rewards, or reinforcements, are not wholly predictable. When we move from the learning laboratory to the outside world, unpredictability is very easy to come by. The more complex an object is, the more different things it can do for you (or you can do with it). That is, the more varied are the reinforcements to which it can lead. Human beings are surely complex

16

"objects," possessing the ability to reinforce in many ways. If a human being can lead to varied reinforcement, and can do so in a largely unpredictable way, then he is capable of becoming a generalized secondary reinforcer. When a person becomes a generalized secondary reinforcer for someone, he is loved by that person.

This generalization covers many types of relationships, all of which are kinds of love. People reinforce each other in many different ways. The different types of reinforcement that prevail in a social relationship are what lead to different kinds of love between people. A mate reinforces one in many ways (hopefully), but they are somewhat different from the ways in which friends reinforce each other. A mother does different things for her children from those a wife does for her husband. In common, all provide a wide variety of rewarding experiences for the other. It follows that "true" love develops after a rather long experience with someone. You cannot develop a history of varied and unpredictable reinforcement from someone instantaneously. Does this preclude "love at first sight?" In a way it does, although, surprisingly, not completely. This phenomenon will be dealt with later.

Love for a person develops when he has been a source of (or simply associated with) many different kinds of rewarding experiences. The variety and unpredictability of the rewards are crucial. If you *know* what kind of reinforcement will come from a person, and when it will come, then you will seek his company only when you want whatever it is you know for certain he will deliver. On the other hand, if you have come to associate someone with a wide variety of pleasant experiences that can come at many different times, then it's natural to seek his potentially pleasurable company most of the time. He is a signal for the possibility of some kind of rewarding event and, hence, you enjoy a state of pleasant expectation when you are around him.

In this scheme of things, you can love good friends and relatives as well as "lovers." So what exactly is the nature of the very real, obvious, and important difference? As mentioned, the main difference is found in the kind of reinforcement that predominates in different kinds of social relationships. One rather apparent difference is that sex, a potent reinforcing agent in many ways, is central in the "lover" relationship.

Sex is not a simple reinforcer. It has varied significance. Certainly the physical pleasure of sexual behavior is a powerful reward, but important as that is, it is not the single most important reinforcing aspect in the development of sexual love. Let's look more fully at the development of erotic love.

### The Development of Heterosexual Love

Our Western culture is based on heterosexual ties. And woven into its fabric is the notion that sexual attractiveness is a most important part of feeling adequate and worthwhile. For years, the mass media of our culture have stressed a rather narrow type of love interaction. It is the handsome dashing hero who gets the heroine, who herself is super attractive and desirable. Sometimes one set of personal qualities is emphasized, sometimes another, but the net result, always, is that personal worth is demonstrated by being sexually attractive to others. It is this proof of adequacy that becomes so reinforcing to us. Since most TV and movie plots seem to concentrate on wooing and winning but not their sequel, the "capture" or attainment is always pictured as the big reward. The physical pleasure that follows is of secondary importance. The point here is that we are taught from infancy that the attention, and possibly even the captivation, of a suitably attractive person makes us adequate, makes us worth something. The more strongly other people view this person as desirable, the more rewarding it is for us to capture him or her. This need, to prove ourselves socially-sexually desirable by attracting others, is important to virtually all of us, and of overwhelming importance to many. Why should this be so?

Most of us, perhaps almost all, harbor some feeling of personal inadequacy, even inferiority. After all, as children, when we were first learning about ourselves and who we are, we were not particularly competent to cope with other people (most of whom were older, bigger, and wiser), or to adequately meet the problems of a very complicated world. Certainly, as we grow older, and become more and more competent to cope with problems, we incorporate these successes as part of our self-image, too. But, we never really completely lose all of the early feelings of inadequacy. The first few concepts that we learn as young children are likely to be vague, broad, and general. Often we cannot cast them into words. They are experienced only as feelings. Later, we may learn other, even contradictory, things about ourselves but these are learned in a more particular way, partly with an assist from language. These self-concepts are more sharply defined. And so the two conflicting learning experiences may never fully collide. The result is that we never completely unlearn many of our broad and general early self-images and feelings. Moreover, early learning tends to be haphazard, that is, very much on a random reinforcement schedule. The last chapter pointed out that this schedule increases the resistance of the learned material to extinction. All of this means that we carry with us into adulthood some inferiority feeling from early childhood. An additional fact that makes these feelings difficult to get rid of is that they are very unpleasant and, therefore, we avoid situations which bring these feelings to mind. This means that we avoid situations which generate inferiority feeling and, of course, that makes it impossible to extinguish these feelings. So we continue to feel inferior, these feelings are unpleasant and they lead to anxiety.

Now if a human being can help relieve these feelings and lower anxiety, he becomes a powerful reinforcing agent. If a very attractive person falls in love with you, or even reveals that he is attracted to you, it is very flattering and it makes you feel good. This encourages you to "approach" this person; to seek his or her company. The interest exhibited by an attractive person of the opposite sex is, then, a powerful reward, and one of the principal sources of reinforcement in the development of heterosexual romantic love.

In childhood or adolescence, most of us form some picture of a desirable mate. This picture may be incomplete, vague, and may incorporate characteristics that, in fact, would make such a person a poor choice for a lifetime partner. For example, the fancied lover may be adventurous, loose, free-wheeling, even irresponsible. It is not altogether unlikely that these characteristics would be attractive to an adolescent. Regardless, the adolescent picture forms a large part of the basis for the attraction others hold for us as adults. So-called "love at first sight" is probably nothing more than the immediate perception that a particular person fits our unconscious image of the desirable love object and is, therefore, capable of making us feel more sexually-socially adequate by returning an interest in us. It is not intended to imply that such is necessarily a poor basis for the beginning of true love. To the contrary, it may very well be the best of all possible beginnings. It should be emphasized, however, that, indeed, it is only the beginning.

True development of love follows upon the initial attraction. Each person must develop the ability to serve as a generalized secondary reinforcer for the other. This cannot happen immediately for it requires time. The couple must build up a substantial history of making the other happy, comfortable, rewarded, etc.; in short, each must become the signal for, or the cause of, many different reinforcements for the other. This, of course, includes, but is not limited to, genuinely making the person feel more adequate. Sincere interest in your partner, a genuine concern for his feelings, an honest respect for his opinions, all make for conditions that help him feel more adequate. This is over and above the initial (and transitory) effect of the first demonstration of being attractive to him or her. It goes without saying that enhancing each other's enjoyment in shared activities, and taking care to please each other in direct ways, contributes to the growing relationship.

Unfortunately, however, many relationships never get that far. One of the most important reasons for this is that some people are virtually incapable of love. Picture, for example, an individual whose feelings of worthlessness are so strong that nothing can shake them. If an attractive potential sex partner then shows interest, instead of concluding that this must prove that he's worthwhile, he immediately devalues that person. Sort of an "If she wants *me*, there must be something wrong with her" response. This self-defeating attitude is not terribly rare, nor is it readily changed. For such people, each new sexual conquest is an empty victory, leading only to the next unsatisfying relationship. In essence, you must value yourself at least a little before you can accept and value someone else's love.

There is recent experimental evidence to support this statement. In a study by Walster (1970), people with low self-esteem tended to devalue highly positive statements made about them as long as there was any possible ambiguity in the situation. People with high self-esteem took ambiguous statements to be flattering. This would lead us to believe that, under circumstances of everyday social interaction (which virtually always involve some degree of ambiguity), high self-esteem people will react with far more positive attitudes toward the two-person interaction than will low self-esteem people. Let's now return, however, to the more nearly "normal" course of events and illustrate, by fictional example, the possible course of development of a love affair. There are certainly many roads to love, and this example is but one. In view of what we know about how people react in such situations, however, it is a most plausible one.

John and Mary are both popular. Each is attractive and socially adept. They meet at a party (where each has a different date). Suddenly they find themselves attracted to each other and they spend a good deal of time (to the neglect of their own dates) flirting and talking. They arrange to meet a couple of days later. Both find the waiting exciting and look forward eagerly to the next meeting. They think of each other a great deal and manage to build up quite attractive images. They meet and drive to some pleasant spot. John is trying to impress Mary and not to disappoint her expectations. He is eager to be just what she wants him to be. Mary is doing exactly the same thing. Voilà—they fit each other's dreams remarkably well. Why not? That's precisely what they're trying to do. They are also bent on finding and sharing pleasure. Perhaps they have a bottle of wine. Both are by now thoroughly infatuated. With each subsequent meeting, the relationship grows more intimate. The more they learn about each other, the more satisfying the relationship becomes. Of course. They are still trying very hard to be just what the other wants, and each is actively engaged in the process of discovering exactly what that is.

This is a truly exciting stage of the relationship. However, it is not based on real knowledge of the other, nor is it stable. Two things are going on. Initially, each judged the other to be sexually-socially desirable and, therefore, their mutual interest was very rewarding. In addition, with help from the other, each has formed an unrealistic and inaccurate picture of the other, one closely matching what each wants the other to be like. Great—but this can't last.

If all goes well during this stage, however, other processes are also taking place. The two are doing things together. They are both getting a large measure of enjoyment out of these things. If they are at all compatible, they are truly enjoying each other's company and building up a large store of shared pleasant experiences. Moreover, the more they realize that they are actually successful in pleasing each other, the better that fact alone will make them feel. Being able to give pleasure to someone who is important to us can be very rewarding. It validates our own worth. Thus, "giving" becomes an important part of the rewards of love.

Inevitably, reality will creep into this relationship. Illusion cannot be sustained forever. Moreover, the thrill of mutual attraction will start to wear off. They will become a little bit more secure in each other's continued interest and, therefore, try a little less hard to continue to impress. This isn't all bad, of course, but it does bring the relationship to a crisis. If there is a large discrepancy between reality and the image, it will be very difficult to overcome the disenchantment. In other words, it is probably good, if the other does fit to some extent, the "adolescent fantasy image" that's been built up, even if the image isn't ideal in some objective sense. The point is, that when reality catches up, love will not survive if the jar to both lovers is severe.

Important in the short term, and even more so in the long one, are the shared experiences of mutual reinforcement mentioned earlier. There are few truisms more accurate than the one that states that true lovers must share many things in common. If there are no common interests, they cannot help each other enjoy many things. However, the basis of a continuing and satisfying love relationship is obviously not all that simple. Interpersonal relationships are complex. People experience many needs, psychological and physical, learned and innate. Other people can help satisfy these needs in many ways. Some of the ways in which we help each other are conscious and deliberate; others arise "spontaneously" out of the fact that we possess certain physical and psychological characteristics; that is, because we are who and what we are.

By "conscious and deliberate" we mean that each partner can deliberately choose to help satisfy the other's needs, to bolster the other's feelings of self-worth and attractiveness. The fading of the original thrill of mutual discovery and infatuation can be replaced by consciously learning how to make the other person feel attractive, adequate, and simply good, about himself. This can be as obvious as praise, or as subtle as paying attention at appropriate moments.

## Love and Honesty

It is most important, with respect to the development of love, that the relationship be basically an honest one. Dishonesty, even in the white lies of flattery, can be seriously damaging. A compliment that isn't sincere is like candy without flavor. It looks good, you reach for it eagerly, only to learn that it's worthless. And it quickly loses its reinforcing property. Eventually, one learns that the other's statements and expressed interest are not always genuine. That person will lose his power to reward you. When your lover tells you that you look very good to him, you give it many meanings. You expect him to be genuinely aroused and pleased by your appearance, to be proud of you, and to want to show you off. If he is casually and insincerely complimenting you, however, this praise, lacking these meanings, will soon become worthless to you.

Honesty also has the effect of making punishment more predictable. This, too, is very important. Just as variety and unpredictability of reward produce approach behavior and encourage efforts to protect the source of these rewards (the basis for love), variety and unpredictability of punishment generate escape behavior and the effort to destroy the source of punishment (the basis for hate). Honestly letting your lover know what you do and don't like about him builds in him the ability to predict accurately the particular circumstances in which he can expect unpleasant consequences. If he can predict these, he can avoid them. If he can't, he may simply avoid you.

An open and honest relationship has other important effects. One grows terribly uncomfortable and anxious when constantly on guard against the lover's "discoveries." On the other hand, if he already knows everything about you, loves you, and accepts you anyway, it is most comforting.

It is quite difficult for most of us to accept the idea that someone can love us despite our inadequacies. Therefore, it's quite difficult to disclose ourselves fully and honestly to another person. The effort is well worth it. Once we accept the fact that someone else can know us intimately and still not reject us (even if there are some things about us he doesn't like), can, in fact, still love us, the feelings of relief, happiness, and comfort with that person are enormously rewarding. It is usually the case, incidentally, that what we perceive as a weakness in ourselves is not so harshly judged by others. Often, one is his own worst critic. Since we are trying in the love situation to build in as many approaches to the love object and as few avoidances as possible, lies and hidden thoughts directly defeat the purpose. To hide something from someone, by definition, you must avoid certain events, perhaps topics of discussion. Quite directly, this introduces avoidance into the relationship and works against the development of approach responses. Moreover, complete honesty makes it very difficult to argue. Think about this a moment. An argument usually contains an element of dishonesty. Most of the time when arguing, we are trying to evoke some response from our "adversary." We are not honestly trying to make clear our own position, we are trying to manipulate, or to gain some concession. We are usually trying to make some kind of impression, or to restructure the relationship. We are not simply trying to clarify and honestly communicate feeling. How much simpler to tell him that something he has done has angered us. This is an honest and open statement of feeling. Usually, this kind of expression averts bitter arguments; arguments that can produce intentional and unintentional punishment, and generate avoidance.

In summary, honesty and openness in a love relationship make it easier to predict (and avoid) punishment from the other person. A dishonest relationship results in unpredictable punishment which can be avoided only by avoiding the other person. Honesty also makes arguments less likely; makes each individual more comfortable with the other because he has nothing to hide; he is accepted for himself. Generally this increases the reinforcing qualities of the relationship. Of course, two people may learn through this openness that they really have characteristics that will make it very unlikely that they can ever love each other. But, clearly it is better to know this early; the earlier, the better.

An open expression of feelings can be reinforcing in itself; can make us feel "clean." In most of our daily relationships we hide our true feelings almost automatically. If we become angry with someone, for example, we seldom tell him. Anger is a powerful emotion and doesn't disappear because we deny its presence. If we don't express it openly and appropriately at the source, then it doesn't simply go away. In fact, suppressing it lends more frustration. This can add to the anger (and to feelings of personal helplessness). In final outcome, anger usually gets expressed at another time, often harshly, maybe indirectly, but almost invariably, inappropriately. The honest statement that someone's behavior has made you angry can relieve your feelings, and when appropriately expressed (not as an attack on the person), will rarely lead to argument.

SUGGESTED READING

For some views of what people have considered important factors in love, we suggest the following brief papers. Chapter IV presents major formal theories of love.

Goode, W. J. The theoretical importance of love. *American Sociological Review*, 1959, **24**, 38–47.

Harlow, H. F. The nature of love. *American Psychologist*, 1958, **13**, 673–685.

Slater, P. E. On social regression. *American Sociological Review*, 1963, **28**, 339–364.

CHAPTER IV

# Psychoanalytic Viewpoints

SUMMARY

The psychoanalytic school, founded by Sigmund Freud, has been most responsible for the early treatment of love in psychological theory. Freud saw love as an expression of sexual desire, learned in a series of five "psychosexual" stages. These stages represent developmental crises wherein the growing human being learns to satisfy his sensual (sexual, in a broad sense) desires within the framework of society. Freudian love, then, is a mechanism in the service of sex.

Erich Fromm and Rollo May have given to classic psychoanalytic doctrine an existential-humanistic direction. Fromm sees love as a striving to overcome the basic state of human loneliness deriving from man's awareness of his separation from the rest of nature. May sees love as the antithesis of the depersonalized, dehumanized, existence of modern man in a technological society. A commitment to another human being is, to May, the means of realizing one's essential human nature.


Throughout the psychoanalytic literature, from the profoundly influential writing of Sigmund Freud to the more recent existential and humanistic productions of Erich Fromm and Rollo May, love and sex have played front stage. This is necessarily so, for an understanding of the human personality, whether well or sick, can be grasped only when sex and love are fully comprehended. Significant observations have been made by the analysts and a number of stimulating ideas generated. The observations have been clinical, however, and rarely scientifically verified. Theory has been woven loosely from individual clinical reports. Each idea, then, must be weighed carefully, for too

26

often, in the psychoanalytic literature, it is difficult to separate observation from fancy and reason from rhetoric. A vagueness of language prevails; the referent becomes quite elusive. Characteristically, basic premises from which the argument is developed are taken to be self-evident. Alternatively, support may be sought in the turn of history, in mythology, or in the unique observation of a single patient. Nevertheless, the contribution of psychoanalysis has been considerable. In spite of the scientific difficulties involved, our understanding of love has been greatly advanced by this effort.

It is the purpose of this chapter to take a brief look at the love thinking of three of the most influential writers of psychoanalytic tradition: Sigmund Freud, Erich Fromm, and Rollo May. Freud founded the position and, until quite recently, his thinking dominated the scene. Fromm and May, while differing with Freud in many ways, have extended the horizons of psychoanalysis and brought the position into the more existential, humanistic, tenor of the second half of the twentieth century.

## Freud and Psychosexual Development

It has been often said that Freud's theory of personality was based exclusively on sex. While a bit of an oversimplification, this evaluation possesses considerable truth. Freud (1933) saw personality development as partly biological and as partly learned; as the unfolding of the sex instinct in the individual as he seeks to express it in many ways, leading finally to the mature fulfillment of heterosexual love. Love, in fact, was looked upon as deriving out of the sex instinct and, thus, in classical analytic theory, love is actually considered to be largely an expression of sex. Our neo-Victorian culture has labored persistently and valiantly to turn this belief around; that is, to define sex as the expression of love. In truth, sex and love can be partners, of course, but we shall hold that discussion for later. For now, let's continue with the views advanced by Freud that relate more or less directly to love.

Freud saw the development of personality as a progression through a series of "psychosexual" stages, each characterized by a different source of pleasure, all broadly conceived of as sexual in nature (more accurately, sensual in nature). These stages, five in number, may be viewed as learning "crises" inasmuch as they reflect the developing child's effort to cope with his elemental needs within his society. The stages are known as: Oral (first year), Anal (second year), Phallic or

Oedipal (third through about the sixth year), Latency (from the sixth through puberty), and Genital (puberty and older). During these stages, the child must learn how to satisfy his needs for food, elimination, interpersonal attraction, social skills, and mature sex, respectively. Freud has described normal developmental progress and he relates the adult's final state of mental hygiene to the degree to which these stages are successfully negotiated.

During the Oral stage (first year of life), pleasure is derived mainly from lip and mouth stimulation; from sucking, biting, and eating. This is the time during which the infant learns not only that oral behaviors are gratifying but that this pleasure results from dependency upon another human being (his mother). Recalling that, to Freud, all pleasure was essentially sexual in nature, this relationship becomes the first source of "sexual" gratification and his mother, the first love object.

During the Anal stage (about the second year), the child first confronts society's strictures. The pleasure he obtains in defecation is, during toilet training, regulated or inhibited by others. He learns that impulse must be controlled and that society will punish him for failure to express himself in an acceptable manner. He also learns that obeying the rules may lead to reward and encouragement.

The Phallic or Oedipal stage (from about the third year through the sixth), is a crucial one in the Freudian position on love. At this time, the primary biological focus of pleasure has shifted to the genital region, the penis in the male and the clitoris (the developmental homologue of the penis) in the female. Now, according to Freud, true sexual yearnings begin to stir. The child develops sexual fantasies featuring the parent of the opposite sex. The development of this early sexual orientation necessarily follows a different course in the male and female child. Freud's account of this sex difference is a bit tortuous and contrived and this aspect of his theory is quite controversial. We shall look briefly at the argument in a moment.

During the Phallic stage, the boy becomes fearful of his mother-directed passive sexual impulses because they bring him into conflict with a powerful rival, the father. These feelings become disturbing, dangerous, even "bad." With the aid of "repression" (thrusting thoughts into the unconscious mind, beyond easy awareness) these feelings and fantasies are denied or avoided, setting the scene for the next psychosexual stage, the Latency period.

The case for the girl is quite different—perhaps more complicated. In a nutshell, she experiences anger and jealousy toward the mother. And she turns to the father as principal love object. Incidentally, to the objection that the analytic account of the Phallic stage seems somewhat bizarre, the devout Freudian rebuts: "But, of course, your personal memories of these events have been repressed and, hence, are unavailable as supporting evidence."

During the Latency period (sixth year through puberty), the child completely avoids his sexual feelings and turns to learning the social and intellectual skills required to cope successfully with social problems. He enters school, the first break with the home, and here is forced to learn to get along with his peers. Somehow, this peer contact readies him for solution to the conflict suffered in the earlier Phallic or Oedipal stage. With puberty, our developing adult is ready to transfer his lust-love to someone of his own age. At this time, the primary source of pleasure again becomes the genital area. And this names the final stage—Genital. Put simply, one might say that the child learns during this period that other people can be instrumental in making him feel good. He also learns that if he does not do things their way, they can withhold or deny him these feelings. He also gets a biological glimpse of the potential for an extremely exciting feeling which he, at first, associates with the parent of the opposite sex. Reality considerations, in the form of social taboos, forbid this, so he transfers this yearning to an age equal of the opposite sex (that is, if all goes well).

To Freud, the great feeling is all a part of sex and the yearning for the satisfying object is love. Thus, love becomes a partially learned desire for a partner of the opposite sex possessing the potential for satisfying this sexual need. The choice of the partner is largely dependent upon just how well he or she becomes a socially acceptable substitute for the parent. In our terms, it is during this stage that the youngster comes to learn about two reinforcing events, the positively rewarding action of sexual expression and the punishing aspects of social condemnation. It is here that our personalities start to take specific shape as we learn our own particular ways to maximize these pleasures and minimize the pain of punishment. Whether it is the positive or the negative consideration that takes precedence at any given time is situationally determined.

It was Freud's emphasis, then, that the child comes to redirect his sexual feelings from the parent of the opposite sex to a socially sanctioned substitute. The notion of parental substitution possesses considerable face validity. It is intuitively reasonable. How often one notes a striking physical similarity between the spouse and the parent of the opposite sex. In view of the infinite variation in physical appearance, this seems an unlikely accident.

Just how the parent of the opposite sex gets adopted as the early love choice is another question. Reasoning from simple learning theory, we would expect that for both the male and female offspring, it is the mother that plays the major reinforcing role, especially in the very early years. The adoption of the mother as the love object would seem to be required of both sexes. The proponents of analytic theory insist that fathers pay more attention to their daughters, while mothers give relatively more attention to their sons. Some evidence for this claim is found in psychological literature.

In the Freudian account, the pitfalls of the Phallic or Oedipal stage differ for the two sexes. At this time the child is supposed to first observe, through some necessary accident, the principal physical difference between boys and girls. Since this discovery entails different perceptions for the two sexes, its effects are different. Recall that, according to Freud, the "lustful urges" of this stage are viewed as dangerous because of competition with the superior rival figure and also that sexual sensitivity is now localized in the genital area. What a shock it is to the boy to discover that some people lack penises! And, in the Freudian account, he attributes this loss to the sin of having expressed overtly the dangerous impulses (inviting a punishment that fits the crime). And he says to himself: "If I am not careful, perhaps daddy will cut off mine." This is the well-known castration fear in the male child in classic psychoanalytic doctrine. It leads to total repression of both the incestuous yearning for the mother and the hostile attitude toward the father. Ignoring his potentially dangerous desires is, of course, the safest course.

The inability to actually consummate sex with the mother, her failure to always instantaneously meet his every need and wish, and maturation, all contribute to this repression. This last factor, maturation, is quite important in determining the ultimate sexual orientation of the person. To Freud (and many others), we are all constitutionally bisexual. In the male, however, the masculine component is stronger and accounts in large part for final emulation of the father and a mature heterosexual preference.

Discovery of the missing penis more or less naturally leads the girl to conclude that the catastrophe has already happened to her. Whereas the male experiences guilt over his sexual impulses toward the mother, and fears castration at the hands of the father, the girl feels angry and blames the mother for the tragic loss of her penis. This serves to weaken the mother's position as love object, a trend that is further enhanced by the conviction that the mother is giving much of her love to others in the family (brothers, sisters, the father, etc.). The girl's love then gets directed toward the father. In part, this occurs because he possesses the cherished organ. There is a touch of envy here and Freud has given this the appropriate title, "penis envy."

Taken together, the castration fear of the male and penis envy in the female are known as the castration complex. This fear in the boy weakens his tie to the mother and launches the quest for her substitute. Given an assist from constitutional factors, this leads him ultimately to the adult heterosexual male role. Penis envy in the girl, on the other hand, encourages jealousy of the mother and love for the father. In "normal" course, however, a relatively dominant feminine constitutional factor leaves her emulating the mother (female role). This identification provides the additional advantage of imagined union with the father as she fancies herself in her mother's place. Her search for the father substitute follows subsequently, since the realities of our society make father, himself, unavailable to her.

The difference between the ways in which boys and girls experience the castration complex should, according to strict analytic theory, result in a heavier burden of guilt in the adult male than in the adult female. Substantial evidence for this is hard to come by. Freud saw a necessary connection between the differing early sexual fantasies and experiences (with a strong nod given to possible constitutional differences) and later differing sex roles. The accepting passivity of the female and the aggressive dominance of the male were more or less ultimate requirements of the theory. It is becoming increasingly apparent that these roles relate more strongly to time and geography. The role difference is dissolving fast in contemporary Western society. This point illustrates well, incidentally, the prevailing criticism of Freud's thinking. It has been widely objected that his clinical observations were narrowly based; that, almost exclusively, he knew a single stratum of society at a particular time in history (Vienna in the early 1900s). And this brings to question the generality of his theory.

## Erich Fromm and the Art of Loving

Fromm's influence begins in the 1940s. As much a social philosopher as personality theorist, he brought to psychoanalysis both a humanistic and existential bent. Freud can be thought of as emphasizing the influence of biology (instinct) on man and on his loving; Fromm sees the culture as the stronger determinant. Neither theorist has totally ignored the other side of the argument, of course.

To Fromm (1956), man is the animal with a problem. Possessing most of the instinctive or biological makeup of animals below him, he possesses, in addition, self-awareness and reason. This leaves him divided, in a state of essential disunity with nature and, as a consequence, he suffers a sense of separateness and loneliness. He copes through love. This assumption is basic to Fromm's position.

Fromm defines love much more broadly than did Freud. To Freud all love derived from sex. Fromm recognizes several forms of love, the erotic being but one. To Freud, love (sex) represented an effort to relieve a state of tension in close analogy to eating or drinking in response to hunger or thirst. Fromm "accentuates the positive;" man becomes human through loving.

To Freud, love of the self and love for others were seen as incompatible. Since the energy of love was thought of as fixed in total amount, love for the self necessarily reduced that available for others. Fromm sees love for the self and love for others as far from incompatible. Rather, they are meaningfully related. It is his insistence that a person cannot love others if he does not love himself.

According to Fromm, man, in his state of loneliness and separation, becomes anxious and seeks union with the world outside him, and with others who make up this world. He makes an effort to "transcend" his life as an individual and attain "at-onement." He may accomplish this in several ways, with varying degrees of success: in orgiastic states, through conformity, through creative activity, or, ideally, through love.

Drug usage, auto-induced trances, and the sexual orgasm are cited by Fromm as examples of orgiastic states. Each reflects a quality of desperation, is transitory in effectiveness, and ultimately fails to close the gap between the individual and the world. The pursuit of the sexual orgasm can become as compulsive in its grip (and ultimately as ineffective) as alcoholism or drug addiction.

In his effort to combat loneliness and separation, the person may surrender his individuality and emulate the "herd" in custom, dress, and the expression of ideas. It is Fromm's conviction that modern man, at least within a democratic form of government, is less compelled to conform by politics than by his own need to get with the world. Conformity generates a kind of equality, but it is the equality of "sameness," not "oneness," and as such, must fail to bridge the chasm. Fromm notes that the equality of conformity is spreading rapidly into the realm of sexual role differences. With the collapse of this polarity, he fears that erotic love will go.

Separateness can also be combatted through creative activity. If the created product genuinely belongs to the individual, that is, results from his personal planning as opposed to the dictates of another, some measure of union with the world is realized. The person becomes a part of his creation and thus dissolves separateness. But, this too is an incomplete solution, for it lacks the personal element. Only through the personal (or interpersonal) can man substantially, and more or less permanently, reduce his loneliness and achieve "transcendence."

Fromm takes as the most powerful and compelling of all man's striving, the effort at "fusion" with another human being. This is the force that holds together man and mankind. And this is what he means by love.

He makes a distinction between mature and immature love. The latter is seen in the symbiotic union wherein there is mutual (and reciprocal) need and dependence. He uses the example, mother and fetus. Unlike the union of symbiosis, mature love preserves the integrity and individuality of the person—both persons. It is an action, not just a passive emotion. And giving takes precedence over taking. Giving, however, is not sensed as suffered deprivation. It is a positive experience. In the sex act, for example, man and woman give to each other in both a physical and psychological exchange. Neither senses loss.

It is Fromm's insistence that the capacity for true giving is found only in the mature personality, one that is free of dependence feelings and the need to exploit others. In the several forms of mature love, four elements predominate: care, responsibility, respect, and knowledge. All of these are requisites and are taken to form a mutually interdependent pattern of broad-scope attitudes.

Care, the first, invites no explanation. To love is to take care of. Responsibility is something else. Implied here is a concern with the psychological needs of the other. Responsibility in the sense intended here is an attitude toward the other that is never duty-bound or duty-dictated; it is given freely. Respect implies dedication to the development of the other one and it presupposes the fourth element, knowledge of the other. Fromm feels that knowledge of the other one, of the self, and, indeed, of man in general, is a kind of by-product of the act of loving.

The desire for union of male and female is perceived by Fromm as both specific and biological. However, just as the union of sperm and egg initiates new birth, so psychological new birth or rebirth occurs in the love relation between man and woman. In true love, the need for union in the two sexes does not represent a simple desire to relieve tension in the Freudian sense. It possesses the positive quality defined by the pattern of basic attitudes described above.

As infant and child, the person experiences only the unselfish love of the mother. The mother's love is given unconditionally, that is, the child is not required to earn it. He gives nothing in exchange. And then, beginning around the age of eight or ten (perhaps earlier), the child starts on the path to mature love. At first, he gives as an exchange product. He gives to receive. Slowly, he comes to mature love. He begins to abandon the use of others to realize his own needs and develops a respect for their needs. His self-centeredness gives way to true giving or sharing; to "oneness" with the other. He makes a transition from loving out of selfish need, to needing because he loves.

In the developmental process, beginning around six years, the father becomes the more significant love object. Unlike the mother's unconditional love, the father's love must be earned. It is conditional. He makes demands on the child and, for this reason, his love may be lost if the child fails to meet his conditions. On the positive side, the child can acquire or earn the love of the father. He can do something about it. He can influence it. The father insists on law and order, on discipline, and on reason. And he offers adventure. Thus, whereas the mother gives the child security, the father gives him the capacity to cope with life's problems.

Fromm emphasizes attitude or character orientation in his analysis of the directions taken by mature love. Narrow attachment to a particular person at a particular time is viewed as immature or symbiotic.

Mature love is generalized; is given freely to all; to "man" and man-kind, not just to one person. Yet, he acknowledges various kinds of love or dominant directions. Thus, there is recognized: brotherly love, motherly love, erotic love, self-love, and the love of God.

Brotherly love is the love of equals, the love for all human beings, the union with mankind. Motherly love is unilateral. The theme is inequality. The mother demands nothing; the child gives nothing. Tradition cites love of mother for child as the highest form of love. It is unselfish and unconditionally given. And it is in this love relation-ship that the child gains security. Fromm speaks of a second stage of motherly love, too often weak or lacking in the mother. The good mother, in her interaction with the child, can also convey a zest for life and living.

Whereas brotherly and motherly love are not directed exclusively toward one person, erotic love is. Erotic love is not to be confused with falling in love or with infatuation. This sudden intimacy is typically short-lived. This intimacy, once achieved, sets the occasion for its own collapse. A fresh lover is sought and, then, like the other, he (or she) becomes too thoroughly known. This union also dissolves. And so it goes. Those who flit from lover to lover never know love in the sense intended by Fromm. Sexual desire is not to be confused with love, for it may spring from many diverse (and irrelevant) emotions such as anxiety, or the need to dominate or be dominated. Sexual attraction (without love) can lead to but momentary, but transitory, union.

Fromm's big point here is this: a satisfying and permanent union between a man and a woman must harbor a strong element of brotherly love. Pure sex won't do it! In the romantic tradition of our times, love is supposed to follow from some sort of irresistible impulse. Not to Fromm. True love must involve the will. It is an act of commit-ment or dedication. And he perceives no contradiction between this view and the commoner assumption that erotic love is a product of unique attraction between one man and one woman. Both hold.

Most of us feel at least a little guilty about self-love. Fromm decries this and views it as arising out of confused early training. But he makes a distinction between self-love and selfishness. It is the latter that is "wrong." The argument is simple and runs like this. The self is also part of the human race. And, as such, is an entirely appropriate love object. True love is generalized. Love all—including the self; otherwise, loving is incomplete. If we cannot love ourselves, we cannot truly love others. The selfish person is one who loves himself too little or not at all. He must wrest from life whatever cheap satisfaction he can immediately put his hands on, for he knows no satisfying love relationships with others.

Fromm relates the love of God directly to the child's love of parents. Its immature expression is seen in those adults who take the view that God is the all-forgiving mother whose love is freely given and unconditional; uninfluenced by the person's faults and foibles. Alternatively, and equally immature in Fromm's view, God is looked upon as the demanding and punishing father whose love is conditional. Mature love of God is found only in the person who has outgrown these childhood attachments, for whom God is no longer a parental substitute. Gone is the sense of helplessness in the face of outside authority. Loving and the exercise of justice have become a part of this person. He has incorporated these principles. The responsibility is now fully his.

There are many ways in which love can go wrong. In fact, in our society, it seldom goes right. Fromm sees the occurrence of true love as a rarity. The "team" relationship found in so many marriages, for example, is perceived as shallow; as devoid of true love. Man and woman simply unite in an effort to bolster one another. Mutual courtesy is the key. And the couple remain strangers to one another. Strongly related is the "sexual marriage" undertaken upon the assumption that perfect sexual intercourse must necessarily foster true love. Technique is the ideal that is pursued. Fromm feels that here the cart precedes the horse. Sexual satisfaction is the by-product of true love, not vice versa. And he decries the influence of Freud (and others) in perpetuating this unhappy delusion.

Then there is "neurotic" love, wherein one or both marital partners have failed to outgrow early feelings for the mother or father. These early attitudes are transferred without alteration to the spouse. For example, the man whose development has been arrested at the stage of childish attachment to his mother seeks unconditional love in his wife. And the wife is soon found short in her giving. Disenchantment and unhappiness follow. True love never even got started. If, on the other hand, the man remains stuck in his early excessive love for, and need to please, the father, it is the wife who must ultimately suffer. She cannot enjoy any central significance to the husband. He is likely to remain aloof in the marriage. His is a constant quest for another "father" or for success. Women play an entirely secondary role in his life; may even be viewed with some contempt. And so it goes. The operation of learning factors is particularly well illustrated in "neurotic" love.

Related to neurotic love are certain forms of "pseudo" love. The person who entertains little regard for himself, who has developed little or no sense of his own integrity and strength, may idolize the partner. He surrenders his own identity and places the partner on a pedestal (from which he or she must ultimately tumble since the role is impossible to carry off).

"Sentimental" love is a further form of "pseudo love." A product of fantasy, the real love union is never even explored. Love becomes a kind of ideal abstraction and is never strained by contact with reality. It is an event holding unlimited promise for the future (or was surely perfect in the past) but never makes it in the here and now.

Fromm does not equate true love with the absence of conflict. He sees most fights between lovers as superficial, as efforts to avoid real conflict. Since these squabbles cover up underlying reality, they cannot be resolved, for they are false. Real conflict, on the other hand, deriving from intimacy, cannot be destructive. Catharsis and ultimate clarification and understanding follow. And each partner is strengthened as a result.

## Love and Will

Rollo May (1970) is an influential writer of existential bent. He feels that the historical determination of emotional illness is of little import. It is the immediacy of the emotional crisis that matters.

He sees modern man as another machine in a machine age. Man has become depersonalized and dehumanized, a victim of his technological culture. He has lost his identity, become anonymous and intolerably lonely. Without feeling, commitment, or involvement, modern man is beset by a numbing apathy; nothing matters. Whereas his capacity to will and to love were once his principal instruments of day-to-day survival, modern man now denies their value and seeks unworkable substitutes. In his personal practice of psychotherapy, May finds it a ubiquitous theme that his patients are unable to will and to love.

May recognizes four kinds of love; five, counting the admixture of the four that he calls "authentic" love. There is sex or lust, eros or creative (procreative) love, philia or brotherly love, and agapé or devotion to the other's welfare. Authentic love combines the four in varying proportions.

Sex and eros engage May's principal interest. These two love forms contrast strongly in his thinking. Broadly conceived, eros is "the urge toward higher forms of being and relationship." Whereas the goal of sex or lust is tension reduction, eros reflects the desire to create or procreate. It is the union of man and woman with passion and feeling; with commitment. It is only through eros that both partners are changed and something new added.

Eros is the basis for tenderness. In our time, says May, eros as a love form is rarely seen. Sex and eros have become totally estranged. Indeed, sex, now practiced so freely on such a broad scale (according to May), is used to avoid or deny eros. The repressed passion of eros often finds expression, however, in behavior that appears (superficially) to be irrational. The couple, entirely sophisticated in birth control, that suffers an "unwanted" pregnancy is, in May's interpretation, carried away by eros. The desire to procreate simply could not be denied.

Sex and modern technology are seen as compatible bedfellows (literally) but not technology and eros. Eros becomes the casualty. Technology stifles passion, spontaneity, and personal identity. Whereas modern man is almost incapable of love, he is obsessed with sex. This obsession, according to May, results in large part from a repressed fear of death. Unable to confront the fact of death or to acknowledge its reality, man turns to sex as the surest demonstration that he is still alive. And the more sex, real or fancied, that he can find, the more undead he is. Hence today's preoccupation with potency.

The relation of love to sex May perceives as paradoxical. Modern man has turned from the puritanical denial of sex that characterized the Victorian period to a new puritanism that admits sex but denies love. The "new freedom" turns out to be no freedom at all. For the diminished cultural restraints of yesterday, man has substituted new shackles fashioned from his overconcern with sexual performance and the demonstration of personal adequacy and sexual technique. He must now play it cool and, as a consequence, his love life has become impoverished, mechanical, and meaningless. Modern man and woman have fallen into a passionless sexual union that is devoid of intimacy and the sharing of the self.

May sees love and will as inseparable. It is will that lends love its substantial and enduring quality. As a negative example, he cites the love movement of the Hippie. Unrestrained, straightforward, and spontaneous, it is nevertheless an expression of love that comes up short. It is indiscriminate; devoid of choice and choosing. Hippie love is passive and instantaneous. True love is an active process, with commitment, and it requires time to grow. It is the act of willing that transforms sex into love. Desire develops out of lust through awareness of the partner and the self and through the act of choosing.

## Comment

Freud made no real distinction between love and sex (lust). He regarded the former as an expression of the instinctual energy of the latter, channeled and shaped by experience. He assigned paramount importance to the notion of psychosexual development and viewed the behaviors manifested during the various stages as efforts to reduce tension. Because of his affirmed determinism, his sensitivity to early environmental influence, and his emphasis upon tension reduction, it has proved feasible to translate his position into contemporary learning concepts. Whether or not Freud would accept these interpretive efforts is, of course, problematical. One of the first systematic analyses of this kind continues, over twenty years later, to be one of the best (Dollard and Miller, 1950).

The tremendous impact of Freud's ideas (entirely revolutionary at the time), combined with later widespread recognition that the supporting evidence that he adduced was less than adequate, has served to encourage others to seek objective validation of his theories. In general, it can be said that this effort has met with little success, one way or the other. This is true largely because most of Freud's hypotheses do not readily lend themselves to the experimental method. One cannot take the castration complex into the laboratory. Experimental studies of animals are feasible, of course, but quite limited in generality. The analogy with complex human love behaviors is simply strained beyond credibility. That leaves surveys, questionnaires, personality tests, and observational studies of children as the principal sources of evidence. The last, observational studies of infants and children, is perhaps, the most promising, and a number of psychologists are currently engaged in this type of study.

Fromm and May share much in common. In their writing, both are more sweeping, or at least less particularistic, than Freud. Love has less a biological determination than a sociocultural one. And, unlike Freud, both view sex and love as two quite different human activities. True love can be known only through "commitment" to the loved one. To both, man's expression of love represents his effort to cope with the anxiety of loneliness. These efforts are healthy or unhealthy, successful or unsuccessful, depending upon the extent to which loneliness-anxiety is reduced. It seems to us that this thinking also fits a tension-reduction model; an interpretation that would be (has been) stoutly rejected by both Fromm and May. Each stresses the positive aspects of true love, which raises again the question of just when is approach not an escape (Chapter II).

Fromm and May are often insightful, often vague, often plausible, and often inspirational. Each has described love more in literary than in scientific terms. However, the formula for achieving ideal love is not readily discerned in their writing. If one accepts the motivational premise that man is driven largely by the anxiety of his loneliness, much, if not all, of the two positions can be fitted into the reinforcement framework of Chapter II. Love behaviors are sustained by anxiety reduction. However, it is not the purpose of our writing to accomplish such a translation.

SUGGESTED READING

Fromm, E. *The art of loving.* New York: Bantam Books, 1963.
Hall, C. S. *A primer of Freudian psychology.* New York: World Publishing Co., 1954.
May, R. Love and will. *Psychology Today,* August 1969, 3, 17–64.

CHAPTER V

# Early Reinforcing Interactions

SUMMARY

To understand adult love relationships, we must understand just what feelings and responses of an approach or withdrawal kind the individual brings into the social situation. What are his attitudes toward others in general? And toward the opposite sex in particular? Is he shy and withdrawn in his approach to others? Or confident and open? Is he willing to risk embarrassment and rejection? Or are his social actions timid and tentative? What are his basic feelings about sex? Is it fun? Or "dirty"? Or, is it okay only under certain well defined conditions? And so on. In the present chapter we explore the old saying that "The child is father to the man." We look at the very early learning of the child that gives shape to the feelings that he holds later about himself, about others, about the opposite sex, and about sex itself.

Some of the more crucial early learning experiences are the initial nurturant interactions with the mother, toilet and sex training, and socialization. Possible effects of these early experiences are related to later interactions with people. In general, if we learn to expect warm and accepting responses in our childhood interactions with people, then we find it easier to accept and return affection in adulthood. Predominantly punitive and harsh upbringings predispose us to a later wary and fearful approach to others. This early learning is in terms of feelings rather than words, and is reinforced in an unpredictable and partial manner. The first fears we learn direct us to avoid anxiety evoking situations, making it difficult to extinguish apprehension.

In general, early reinforcing interactions, both positive and negative, between parent and child, are highly instrumental in the child's formation of the feelings and behaviors likely to prevail in his adult relations to others.

41

Chapter II pointed out that a stimulus, be it a flashing light or a fetching woman, can come to evoke a pleasurable expectancy when it is associated with a rewarding experience (pleasurable stimulation or relief from discomfort). We named the pleasurable expectancy "hope," and we called the stimulus a "hope signal." It was said that we tend to approach hope signals, and that these signals and the approach behaviors that go with them, become very powerful, indeed, when the signal has been associated frequently but unpredictably with many different kinds of rewarding experiences.

Chapter III applied these principles in an analysis of adult heterosexual love with the principal focus on an imaginary love affair between John and Mary. It was shown just how two individuals can come to attract and hold each other; that is, love each other. John's actions frequently rewarded Mary. Mary's actions frequently rewarded John. As a consequence, the sights and sounds of each became hope signals for the other. Each became the love object of the other. And each came to approach the other at every opportunity. It is our purpose now to examine much earlier love behavior. We must look to infancy and childhood to discover the origins of their love affair. Love experienced as an adult is, in large part, a matter of generalization from what we learned as infant and child. To fully understand it, then, we must describe the learning experiences of the infant and child that establish very early love. In doing this, we shall be guided in part by the thinking of the psychoanalysts (Chapter IV).

We come to love another human being when his actions serve to reward or reinforce us many times and in many ways. It is in this way that the other can become a love object or the generalized hope signal that we approach in thought and action. In order to understand how people can act as reinforcing agents, we must take a look at what people want; that is, we must consider the problem of motivation. Here lies the answer to the question of just how *any* event can reward or reinforce.

Traditionally, psychologists have talked about motivation in terms of likes and dislikes, wants, urges, desires, interests, motives, needs and drives. Some of these "well springs of action" are clearly unlearned; some are learned. Hunger and thirst are examples of the former; anxiety and ambition, the latter. And it has been widely assumed that reinforcement gets its value from the existing motivational state. If we are not thirsty, water lacks reward value. If we are not hungry, food cannot reinforce. If we possess no interest in sex, the passing girl doesn't turn us on. If we are not anxious, reassurance from another becomes so much meaningless verbiage. If we don't want riches, money doesn't control our behavior. And so it goes. Reinforcement presupposes motivation. We shall refer to these motivational states as drives or needs.

## Motivation and Reinforcement in Infancy

A great deal of learning takes place in infancy, far more than the typical parent is aware of. It is an unusual kind of learning, for the infant lacks language. He cannot label his experiences or cast them into symbolic representation. Presumably, he learns almost exclusively in terms of feelings and various sorts of images. Further, his very early repertory of skills is restricted to thrashing about, crying and, a bit later, smiling. These are his only means of influencing his environment, of getting action out of the adult who acts as his caretaker.

As infants we experience many intense and recurring sources of discomfort. Foremost is hunger. But there is also colic, the wet diaper, the cold room, or the hot room, the bright light, and the like. Collectively, these are usually called comfort needs. As infants we are totally helpless to cope with them. We begin life with a full dependence on other human beings. This dependence continues for a long time. It is many years before the human being becomes more or less adequate to cope successfully with his needs, unassisted by another. This early experience of helplessness probably establishes at least some sense of personal inadequacy and inferiority. It marks the beginning of a learned need for approval and acceptance. Present in some degree in all of us as adults, this need lends a powerful reinforcing quality to the actions of the lover who gives recognition, approval, and acceptance.

The human agent who relieves the infant's discomfort will become a very powerful hope signal. Let's illustrate this. The infant grows hungry and cries. The crying arouses concern in the mother. She presents the breast or the bottle. The eager infant seizes the nipple. Relief is under way. In the first year of life, this particular reinforcing interaction with the mother occurs perhaps 2000 times. And this describes but one such positive interaction. How many times does she cuddle and fondle the infant? How often does she remove the wet diaper, arrange cover against the cold, discover the open diaper pin, etc? Given such an extensive and intensive association with the relief of the infant's comfort needs, the mother has got to become the first love object. This point is obvious. Less apparent is the fact that the infant is at the same time forming basic attitudes toward "society," that is, toward human beings in general and, perhaps, toward womanhood in particular. The mother is almost the total society of the infant. She is the first "other one." If her actions are largely rewarding, the basis for trusting and approaching others in adulthood (so essential to the first stage of a love affair) has a beginning. Some authorities contend that, in the first year, social attitudes are firmly fixed for life. Usually, but not always, the mother's actions are predominantly of this positively reinforcing kind and she becomes a powerful hope signal. Even the sight of the mother approaching may, sooner or later, come to exert a calming influence as a pleasurable expectancy takes over. Relief is near.

Both Erich Fromm and Rollo May (Chapter IV) have assumed that the basic human condition is one of loneliness. And loving is the means of relieving this loneliness. Twenty years ago, Dollard and Miller (1950) offered an entirely plausible learning account of loneliness. They showed us just how the condition of loneliness could become established in infancy in the reinforcing interaction of mother and child. The principles they employed at the time are quite similar to the principles used by the present writers.

Dollard and Miller pointed out that it is when he is alone that the infant suffers the most severe distress. In the absence of the caretaking mother, the helpless infant suffers mounting discomfort. His hunger grows and his distress may be further exaggerated by the painful feedback from his own vigorous crying. The presence of the mother then brings relief. She becomes a hope signal. And through generalization, the child comes to view all others as hope signals. The basis is laid for later seeking the company of other human beings. In their presence, safety and hope are felt. In their absence, apprehension, for he has learned that pain may follow.

This is, of course, an example of discrimination learning and it seems quite reasonable to assume that the early events of infancy could so conspire as to establish in all of us, in varying degree, of course, the feeling of loneliness that is so much a part of the clinical observations of Fromm and May. This condition might be described as a learned drive, and it forms a major part of the motivational basis for the powerfully reinforcing experience of receiving acceptance from another as adults.

Obviously, reinforcement can go the other way, too. If the mother is associated more strongly with increasing discomfort, she may establish herself as a learned negative reinforcer; she comes to signal fear. This may happen with an unwanted child. The mother handles the infant roughly, ignores his crying, or, perhaps, leaves him half hungry much of the time. The sight and sound of her come to arouse apprehension. She has become a secondary negative reinforcer. And the basis is laid for negative feelings toward all others. The adult, so treated in infancy, is likely to experience great difficulty in making the initial approach response to other people. This early apprehensive response can persist into maturity to adversely affect love in many other ways as well. The occurrence of this apprehension is the more bewildering and painful to the victim at that time because of the absence of memory (words) for the infantile learning experience.

The apathy of modern man, strongly stressed by Rollo May (Chapter IV), can be viewed as a further consequence of early maternal neglect. And, again, it was Dollard and Miller (1950) who first proposed a cogent learning analysis.

The chronically neglected infant is a loser from the start. Regardless of his actions, reinforcement is not forthcoming. His efforts at securing the relief of comfort needs always fail. What little he is equipped to do, crying, kicking, thrashing about, for example, earns him nothing. His distress continues. He learns only that he is powerless. He cannot influence his world. And the beginning of a "What's the use?" attitude is established.

This kind of learning may occur for the first time with weaning. Here, even the nurturant mother fails to reinforce because of the demands the culture imposes on her. Her natural impulse may be that of responding instantly to the cry of her infant but, often, she has been taught to think differently: "He's got to learn to give up the bottle." She withholds reinforcement and the occasion is set for the learning of a sense of helplessness as the child fails in his vigorous entreaties. Mama keeps her jaw set.

In sum and substance, this section tells us that the early interaction of infant and mother can be crucial in establishing the basis for the social attitudes that later govern our approach or withdrawal from others. If the mother acts promptly to relieve the infant's comfort needs, she becomes an adored love object. The infant will develop warm feelings toward her, toward womanhood, and toward other human beings in general. And adult heterosexual love has the best of all beginnings. How fortunate this baby. And how rare. Unhappily, mothers are imperfect reinforcing machines. They, too, possess needs, and needs that do not always dovetail smoothly with the infant's demands. Reward is sometimes delayed or withheld. The hope signal is weakened.

At the extreme, the mother can become a fear signal. If associated more or less constantly with mounting distress, she comes to arouse apprehension and escape behavior. Count on difficulties for this individual in his later love life.

### Socialization and Punishment

Socialization of the human being necessarily introduces punishment. The strictures imposed on the developing child by society almost always run against the grain of his natural impulses. Punishment enters as the means of establishing the taboos that society holds sacred. This begins with the weaning process. But it is in the areas of toilet training and sex training that the thumbscrews are applied. Custom dictates where the developing child must empty his bladder and bowels, and what and who constitute proper objects of love. It is the parents, of course, who must train him in these proper ways. They must apply punishment, for the natural actions of the child in these two areas are behaviors that society forbids. These behaviors must be inhibited and the child must substitute approved conduct.

Society requires the parents, first the mother and a bit later the father, to bring to bear punishment. This often begins as early as the second year of life. Ideally, punishment should be held to the minimum required to discourage the occurrence of the forbidden behavior, permitting the approved behavior to take place. The latter can then be rewarded. Bear in mind that punishment can only teach us what not to do. We must still learn what to substitute. This point is an important one. Let's illustrate in some detail just what we mean.

Our society requires of the child that sooner or later he must learn to use the toilet. He should urinate and defecate in a particular place. His natural impulse is far different from this, of course. Distress arising within him urges immediate relief. It says to him, do it now and here. To substitute the approved behavior he must first give up the immediate response. If the mother begins to punish him for his errant actions, this will establish inhibition, all right, but that's only half the battle. He has simply learned not to urinate; not do it here and now. Punishment has the effect of causing him apprehension when he feels the urge within him. So he restrains himself, at least momentarily. He has not yet learned to go to and use the toilet. The mother must guide him. This is usually accomplished by physically placing him on the toilet at frequent intervals, setting the occasion for rewarding socially acceptable behavior. The mother can and should now apply reward. Notice that in toilet training, the mother has played a dual role. First she punished the child and then she rewarded him. It's hardly surprising that, in the child's mind, her signal value is a bit mixed up. Ideally, in all this, she has become more of a hope than a fear signal.

The reader should be reminded at this point that we are describing the early formation of the social attitudes that will likely prevail later in life. Early response to the mother will probably be carried into adult life to become the response to other women and to other people in general.

Toilet training can go sour in many ways. If the mother punishes severely and often, and especially if she starts training too early, she becomes the fear signal that can, through generalization, adversely affect the love relationships of later life. Dollard and Miller (1950) are particularly lucid on this point. They suggest that, if toilet training is begun too early, the child experiences great difficulty in forming the required discriminations. Punishment is likely to be associated with the mother as such rather than with his own internal signals. He doesn't see just what is wrong. Sometimes the mother's disgust with the dirty diapers is seen by the child as disgust or loathing for him. Thus, the basis for feelings of unworthiness has a beginning. The self-concept is damaged. This analysis possesses intuitive appeal and does not contradict what we know about learning. If this inferiority feeling does develop, one can well imagine the effect it may have on a burgeoning love affair. If the individual brings to it a deep sense of unworthiness, it will become impossible for him to accept positive feelings. An important later consequence of low self-esteem was brought out in Chapter III. The individual who has succeeded in attracting a member of the opposite sex may downgrade that individual. Since he feels unworthy if this attention, it follows that the one granting him this must be essentially worthless in the first place. This is hardly an ideal beginning for love.

A related effect on later behavior is the possible consequence of oversevere cleanliness training, especially if applied too early. This may establish the basis for later timidity in social relationships. If the child cannot clearly relate his particular "misbehaviors" to the occurrence of punishment, he becomes chary of all risk taking. Initiative on his part becomes dangerous. This socially crippling attitude will be broadened and strengthened by parents who impose severe restrictions on the child's later exploratory activities. Fearful that he will dirty up the house or injure himself, these parents further encourage passivity and inaction by making the world pretty much a dangerous place to live in. This child is likely to show little self-confidence in adult social relationships. Later risk taking, essential in the love relationship, comes hard.

Sometimes a kind of vicious circle develops in the toilet training situation. The child may eventually come to rebel and exhibit aggressive behavior toward the frustrating parent. This, of course, invites additional punishment. Further, the rebellion sometimes takes the form of stubborn refusal to defecate when placed on the toilet. This not only brings on even more punishment but also has the unfortunate effect of delaying the very response that could bring about positive reinforcement. Tricky indeed is the right course to be steered by the mother as an ideal reinforcing machine.

Rebellion and the show of aggressive behavior toward the parents presents a big problem in its own right. It is a rare child that does not sooner or later turn against the parent who punishes him frequently and severely; who, in other words, acts to constantly frustrate him. Frustration triggers rage, and rage calls for action. If the expression of rage is punished also, and this is often the case in our society, especially in middle-class families, the child may develop what Dollard and Miller (1950) have called anger-anxiety. He becomes apprehensive when he feels himself getting angry.Carried into adult life in extreme form, this will adversely affect all but the coolest social relationship.

The intimate interaction of two people necessarily introduces some degree of individual frustration. One can never have his way totally. Indeed, were this true of the relationship between a man and a woman, we'd have accommodation, not love. Often, anger is justified and should be expressed honestly and overtly. A meaningful love relationship will survive this; will probably be improved by it. Far more damaging is the continued seething of the person unable to give vent to his angry feelings.

No behavior is more rigidly regulated in our society than the expression of sex. And in no other instance is the "right behavior" more strongly subject to delayed reward. Like toilet training, early sex training relies heavily on the application of punishment which, again, becomes the parents' *modus operandi*.

Although the capacity to reproduce waits on puberty, sexual urges occur quite early in life, much earlier than most parents are willing to recognize. For example, masturbation in the first year of infancy is by no means a rare thing. Sensitivity in the genital area is there, as is a developing capacity to manipulate objects. The exploratory behavior of the child then easily leads him to masturbatory activity. This arouses anxiety in the mother who has made society's masturbation taboo a part of her conscience (first taught her in her own childhood). She punishes the child in an effort to discourage this behavior. And so it goes with other early "deviant" expressions of sex. In her management of the child's early sex life, the mother runs all the risks associated with toilet training, and then some. Again, she gives a potent beginning to the social attitudes and feelings that will later govern approach to, or withdrawal from, people in general. But she also teaches something else. She teaches the child particular feelings about, and responses to, sex as such. These feelings and responses attain future importance, of course, in the love relationships of maturity. Because it is generalized into adulthood, this early learning can make or break love. Too often parents put across to the child a strong conviction that sex is "dirty." That lesson, learned well, pretty much guarantees an unhappy adult sex life.

An unfortunate fact is associated with early sex training. The parents cannot positively reinforce the approved substitute behavior. They can only teach restraint and inhibition. Through the application of punishment, they can only insure that the child will develop apprehension when he feels the impulse to masturbate, or to make sexual approach to a member of the same sex or to a member of his own family, for example. And the child may apply the check rein (or at least give up the public practice of these activities). But, the opportunity to make the "right" response is lacking. The socially sanctioned behavior that must be ultimately substituted for the tabooed activity, lies far in the future. Thus, he cannot turn from his guilt feelings about, say, masturbation, to immediate sexual intercourse with an unrelated member of the opposite sex under the comforting umbrella of marriage. This makes early sex training almost exclusively an exercise in punishment and fear learning. At the very best, given some language development, the child may come to accept as a substitute the vague promises of future sex rewards offered by the parents. Just why so few of us are completely at ease with sex as adults is certainly no mystery. Early training is admirably suited to the establishment of guilt feeling over almost all sexual expression.

## Sex Typing

Sex typing, the adoption of the male or female role, is an important aspect of early socialization. When one considers the everyday, garden variety type of learning pressure brought to bear on the child to shape his identification with the right sex, the Freudian account, outlined in Chapter IV, seems strained indeed. As parents, we begin by labelling the child with a proper male or female name. Then we pick the right hair style, the right clothes, the right toys, and the right play activities. Whereas the very early confusion of the child in his sex identification may amuse the parents at first, this soon gives way to extensive training procedures designed to set the child right. In all of this, the boy is subjected to much stronger pressures in the direction of masculinity than the female in the direction of femininity (Brown, 1958). Girls are permitted much wider latitude in their choices of clothes, of toys, and of play activities. Contrast the difference in parental reactions to the girl's wearing pants and the boy's wearing a dress, or to the girl's interest in a BB gun versus the boy's excitement over dolls. This even extends to names. There are far more female Jackies, Billies, and Jos than male Sues. Tomboyism is mildly discouraged, sissyism is crunched.

The father is typically more concerned with sex typing than the mother, and he is likely to view the slightest homosexual sign in the boy with something only slightly short of horror. He applies reward and punishment, both direct and indirect, in an effort to eliminate the boy's confusion on this score. Considering the depth and extent of this early training, it is really a bit surprising that overt homosexuality has any appreciable frequency in the adult male population of our society. And it is no accident that case histories of adult male homosexuals often reveal an early childhood devoid of strong masculine influence. The father is either absent or meek and submissive in his relationship to the wife (and mother). The latter often continues into adolescence and even maturity as the dominant parent figure.

There is considerable evidence that the female in our society winds up with greater confusion about her sex role than does the male (Brown, 1958). By itself, the greater flexibility of roles permitted in childhood could account for this. But there is another good reason. The male enjoys a privileged position in our culture. This begins early in life and so does the girl's awareness of this unfavorable comparison. At all ages, far more females than males express a preference for the role of the opposite sex. This marked contradiction between what she should or can be, and what she prefers as a sex role, probably contributes heavily to the woman's confusion and conflict in sex typing.

During World War II, society's insistence that "the place for the woman is in the home," gave way in a confrontation with the manpower shortage. Breaking with the feminine tradition, women in large numbers moved to the assembly line and the military desk job. The trend (actually beginning early in the 1900s) has continued ever since. With the wife now a frequent figure in the professional or business world, the husband has reevaluated his position on the domestic scene. He has picked up the dish rag and the mop or, for the first time, entered into a significant caretaking relation to the children. This all adds up to a growing convergence of the two sex roles. Convergence is under way and it's here to stay. And it's unlikely that the collapse of dress and hair styling differences that characterize today's youth will mark the end. The ultimate impact on child-rearing practices and on the incidence of homosexuality is anybody's guess. Enough data aren't in.

SUGGESTED READING

Dollard, J., & Miller, N. E. *Personality and psychotherapy*. New York: McGraw-Hill, 1950. Especially Chapter X.

Mussen, P. H., Conger, J. J., & Kagan, J. *Child development and personality*. New York: Harper and Row, 1963. Especially Chapters 6 and 7.

# CHAPTER VI

# Love and Sex

SUMMARY

Sex presents several physically rewarding aspects that can contribute significantly to love's growth. In addition, there are emotional satisfactions, such as the personal acceptance implied by sexual surrender, that serve as further sources of positive reinforcement. In general, however, our culture fosters mixed feelings and attitudes about sexual behavior. And these can detract from the positive effects.

Need for intimacy, both physical and emotional, are characteristic of love. The closeness of the sexual act can help meet these needs. Love and sex thus enhance each other.

Insofar as we believe that sex is immoral, our enjoyment of sex, of ourselves, of love, and of life, all suffer.

Sex is complex, a primary physical reinforcer, and vastly more. Let's take a closer look. In spite of the great popular interest in sex, or, perhaps in a way, because of it, it has been only recently that we have gathered any substantive knowledge of human sexual behavior. The work of Kinsey and his collaborators (Kinsey, Pomeroy, and Martin, 1948; Kinsey, Pomeroy, and Gebhard, 1953) represented the first major attempt to study this topic in a scientific manner. And it has been only quite recently that scientists have investigated the physiological mechanisms involved in the human sexual act and shared their findings with us (Masters and Johnson, 1960; 1966). Prior to these studies, few people denied that sexual intercourse was a primary reinforcer, but other than the fact that people seemed to enjoy it, and that it sometimes made babies, very little was actually known about it. The partially tabooed topic of sex had been much

52

discussed but little studied. Speculation was rampant and dogma king. For example, as late as the middle 1960s, even the physiological mechanism for so basic a response as vaginal lubrication was universally misunderstood. We have also only recently learned that coitus can be usefully viewed as having almost distinct stages, and under favorable circumstances, an orgasm can involve a dramatic response of virtually the entire body (Masters and Johnson, 1966).

The recent explosion of knowledge in this realm is important and interesting, but largely beyond the scope of this book. The suggested readings at the end of this chapter will provide the reader with a fuller discussion of the topic. For now, we shall discuss only those points which are immediately relevant to our understanding of the relationship(s) between love and sex. A central question for us is: "What aspects of sexual behavior are reinforcing?"

*The Reinforcements of Sex*

A positively reinforcing event usually reduces some drive. Obviously, a sexual orgasm reduces a drive; and an orgasm is reinforcing or rewarding in every sense in which we've used the terms. People will learn to approach those things which lead to sexual orgasms. Since this usually entails positive interaction with some other person we should be able to conclude that successful sexual intercourse will lead to a reinforcement of approach responses to the sexual partner. Our culture does not operate in quite so straightforward a fashion, however, since sex itself is invested with many psychological meanings. Before we turn to an analysis of these meanings, it is relevant to ask whether there are reinforcing elements in sexual intercourse other than the orgasm.

It was mentioned in Chapter V that simply cuddling, petting, and making contact with the skin are reinforcing events, largely primary, that contribute to the early mother-infant "love affair." Sexual intercourse, then, must be invested with this type of reinforcement. In addition, there is experimental evidence that intercourse that fails to culminate in an orgasm is, itself, a powerful reinforcer (Sheffield, Baker, and Wulff, 1951). Experimenters separated copulating rats before they finished. The male animals thus treated could be trained to run down an alley with the only reward being incomplete copulation; they never experienced an orgasm.

The reinforcing value of copulation sans climax probably surprises no one. Introspection will reveal the pleasurable (or approach) properties of the sexual act, even without orgasm. In view of the fact that a significant number of people, primarily women, experience various degrees of difficulty in obtaining sexual climax, this is most important. It suggests that sexual intercourse may be reinforcing to both partners, even if one or both fails to achieve an orgasm. We are in no way attempting to deny, of course, that an orgasm vastly increases the reinforcing aspects of the sexual act.

The female's difficulty in achieving orgasm has been a much discussed phenomenon. Its importance to us lies in the fact that orgasms have been frequently related to psychological factors. Freud, for example, insisted that mature female sexuality involved the ability to experience a vaginal orgasm (as opposed to a clitoral orgasm). He asserted that women who do not climax during the course of conservative copulation (involving only penile-vaginal stimulation) are psychologically immature, that is, neurotic. The view that only the vaginal orgasm is "normal" has survived until quite recently. Indeed, it may still be alive.

For example, a psychiatrist writes:

"At any rate, whenever a woman is incapable of achieving an orgasm via coitus, provided the husband is an adequate partner, and prefers clitoral stimulation to any other form of sexual activity, she can be regarded as suffering from frigidity and requires psychiatric assistance." (Caprio, 1953, p. 78).

We now know, however, that the clitoris is the primary site of female sexual excitement (see, for example, Masters and Johnson, 1966). It is also true that with many couples, conventional sexual positions do not afford the woman adequate clitoral stimulation. We are forced to wonder how many women have felt inadequate, anxious, and even guilty, because of this widespread misconception stemming from analytic theory.

Making matters worse, we know that anxiety of this type actually interferes with the ability to achieve an orgasm. (Anxiety can upset the delicate balance of the autonomic nervous system which is necessary for a fully successful sexual experience. See Chapter XII.) Many women are made anxious about their failure to climax through what are, for them, inadequate means. This anxiety then feeds the problem, and the sex act is made more tense and difficult. In this way, an aversive component is added. On top of this, should this failure and tension continue for any length of time, the woman will invite the label, "frigid." This word, which has become a heinous insult, can do little but engender further anxiety and further escape behavior. What are the potential effects of this on love?

*Sex and Love*

The relationships between love and orgasm have engendered flights of fanciful assertion. Some authors, for example, have suggested that a complete orgasm is not possible unless the sexual partners are "in love" with each other (Reich, 1942; Lowen, 1965). In answer to this, we can say that measured orgasmic responses to stimulation by mechanical penises have produced physically spectacular orgasms (Masters and Johnson, 1966). The definition of orgasm would thus have to be stretched beyond acceptable limits to maintain that love was necessary to produce it. Clearly, love can increase sexual pleasure, undoubtedly even the pleasure of the orgasm itself. We shall argue this very point at greater length later. But what we are emphatically stating is that sex and love are neither the same thing, nor even inextricably tied together.

Although love is surely not necessary for sex, the desire for sex is an almost definitive part of what we call, in Western culture, "romantic love." Excitement and arousal in our lovers' presence is a component of our fantasy of true romance. As a consequence of this, we tend to interpret divers sorts of physiological arousal as romantic feeling when it is experienced in the presence of an attractive member of the opposite sex (Walster and Berscheid, 1971). Thus, almost anything that causes the adrenaline to flow can enhance the feeling of love, at least temporarily.

This principle can explain some apparent contradictions in romantic feeling. If we experience fear with a potential lover, we often tend to find ourselves more strongly attracted to him afterward. For one thing, the fear *reduction*, which follows the aversive feeling of fear, is highly rewarding. For another, the physiological arousal can be interpreted as sexual excitement, especially in retrospect. And so we have the phenomenon of the roller coaster ride at the amusement park.

In addition, as many couples know, a lovers' quarrel can end in a most gratifying embrace. Anger, too, is a stimulant.

Returning to the effects of sexual experience on love, sexual relationships, particularly those leading to orgasm, should certainly contribute to the development of love for the sexual partner. Although
this statement, simply put, is true, the situation is rarely that simple
in our society. Obviously, we still have many hangups left over from
the Victorian era. There is still, for example, the feeling that sex
must be justified in some way. The enjoyment of both giving and
receiving sexual pleasure is not sufficient justification in the eyes of
many people. Sex, it is felt by some, is inherently immoral, and
therefore requires some external justification in order to be indulged
in. Perhaps this attitude was once meaningful. It helped to introduce
the permanency required for the rearing of children. This purpose has
become obsolete, however, with the advent of methods of separating
sex from procreation. It is often argued, though, that this is changing;
that we are undergoing a revolution in our sexual attitudes. What
is the evidence for this?

*Sexual Revolution?*

A typical example of apparent change in attitude has been termed
the "new morality" (e.g., Hettinger, 1966) based on interpersonal
growth and love. Hettinger, a cleric, purports to hold a modern view
of sexual behavior. He still decries free sexual exercise, but not, apparently, for the same old Victorian reasons. Instead, he limits sex
to a situation wherein the young man can insure ". . . that sex will
express his (and the girl's) deepest longings and emotions rather
than a purely superficial and selfish lust" (Hettinger, 1966, p. 43).
But what is the rationale for requiring even this test? Would he
consider placing an analogous requirement on some other biological
drive such as hunger? Must every meal be a banquet or nothing?
Obviously, there is still some feeling that sex is not just a normal
biological drive, but rather that it requires some special justification.
It must express "deepest longings."
In similar vein, the Kronhausens (1960, pp. 227, 228) quote a young
college boy as an articulate spokesman of the "new morality":

"To sleep with a girl I do not love and who does not love me,
even if she willingly agrees on a perfectly rational basis, is wrong,
for these reasons: (a) Any casual relationship goes against the feeling
ingrained in me from childhood that sex and love are inextricably

combined. If I find they can be separated too easily and satisfactorily, it will take something away from my feelings about the relationship I will have with the girl I marry. It could also set up in me a habit pattern leading to later infidelity, a thing that would be destructive to my marriage relationship. (b) It violates her personality. Any girl's value to the man she wants to marry is cheapened more and more, the more boys she has slept with before him.

"If we deeply love one another and find in sex a way of showing its deepest levels; if we find that during and after and because of it we are both striving to grow in stature in each other's eyes; if we find that because it is loving, the release of the sex energy also releases, rather than uses up, our deepest creative energies; if each time there is a sexual interlude, we find we love and respect and admire each other more afterwards, then, and only then, but so sensitively and wonderfully then, it is right."

There are many facets to this statement. It expresses well many of the less rational but commonplace feelings about sex. The young man states that he has been reared to feel that sex and love are "inextricably combined" and he defends this article of faith by saying that the consequences of finding it to be untrue will damage future relationships with the girl he will marry. He then pronounces (but this time evidently feels that no defense of the statement is necessary) that sexual experience will lower the girl's value to her future husband. Most of all, however, the statement clearly reflects, and attempts to defend, the ingrained belief that sex, for its own sake, is inherently wrong. This heritage of our culture results in a detrimental effect on the reinforcement value of sex, interfering with its potentially great capacity to assist in the development of love. This is quite the opposite of what is evidently intended by the rationalization of the "new morality" in which sex is supposed to be something special, reserved only as a contributor to love. Is this too harsh a judgment of the "new morality"? Perhaps we should explore it further.

Sex is presented as wrong and destructive unless it is associated with love. This means, of course, that a couple must be in love prior to having sexual experience with each other, thus removing a potentially major source of reinforcement from the early development of the relationship. The prohibition of loveless sex can have additional damaging effects. Whether we are in love or not, sex remains a compelling biological urge. The frustration of this drive, then, can certainly become an aversive component in the relationship. Since love is seldom well defined in most people's minds, what simpler resolution of this conflict could there be than for people to convince themselves that, in fact, they are in love. It follows that sex is all right. Once again this seems to defeat the intent of the "new morality." Love becomes a false excuse for sex. This scarcely enhances love; apparently, it produces precisely the situation that the "new morality" seeks to avoid. That is, it makes sex the primary determinant of whether or not people believe themselves to be in love.

Moreover, people who are reared to believe that sex is inherently wrong are going to find it difficult to suddenly lose this perception when they are in love, married, or at any other time. Put another way, if we learn an aversive reaction to the stimulus of sex, the highly symbolic difference in the situation (now you're "in love" so it's good and wholesome) is not easily sensed. If we can't clearly discriminate this "new" situation from the one we've learned to avoid (or at least feel anxious and guilty about), then, obviously, we shall experience at least some of these same negative reactions to sexual stimuli even when it's supposedly all right. This conflict, then, also detracts from the positively reinforcing properties of sex. Once more, its value as a developer of love is weakened. In spite of all this, sex remains a powerfully reinforcing event, both physically and emotionally.

So far we have discussed primarily the physical aspects. The positive emotional values of sex may be even more important. It has been pointed out that acceptance by another human being is a very powerful reinforcer. Sexual surrender represents one of the fullest ways in which we can show acceptance of another. In a sense, this is one way in which the societal morality has some effect in the intended direction. The fact that sex is invested with strong cultural taboos means that the willingness to break these taboos (especially a female's willingness) must indicate a very high degree of acceptance of another. This is not, however, an unmixed blessing. Remembering the statement quoted by the Kronhausens, we note that this feeling is an important part of the young man's rationale, that is, "cheap" sex is undesirable—sex should be reserved for highly emotional, highly special and, of course, highly tense situations. One result of this can be seen in the phrase "each time" in the quote above. This young man believes that every single sexual contact must somehow be a symphony of spectacular emotionalism. This naive belief, shared to some extent by many people, has wreaked much damage. In view of the intricacies of human life, in view of the very emotional (both positive and negative) nature of sexual behavior that this attitude relies on, it is absurd to believe that each act will be a totally beautiful and growing experience. This amount of tension surrounding the act, increased by the unreal attitude that every contact must be superb, may increase anxiety in the entire relationship—actually contributing to its destruction. The net result of all of these tendencies is that sex in our culture has assumed on the one hand, an exaggerated importance (emotionally), and on the other hand, has lost some of its pure and powerful physical reinforcement value.

Thus the confusion of sex and love, from Freud to Hettinger, has been detrimental to the enjoyment of both behaviors. The only positive benefit we find here is in the increased meaning that sex takes on as a symbol of acceptance; but even this seems a mixed blessing.

Logical extensions of the argument limiting sex to love would place a high value on the "gift" of chastity to the lover. (As part of the double standard, this gift is considered far more important when the chastity is the female's.) Stripped of its culturally determined emotional value, this gift of inexperience hardly seems an advantage. Few men would welcome with enthusiasm the "gift" of the first meal his wife (or lover) prepares him. It seems, therefore, that the only reason that this can be valued is because it represents at least partially forbidden behavior, and thus involves a willingness to defy cultural mores in order to exhibit depth of love. With the disadvantage of increased tension, a high price indeed is paid for this "gift." Arguments for a truly more liberal morality are made eloquently by the Kronhausens (1960; 1964) and by Albert Ellis (1958). (See the suggested readings at the end of the chapter.)

This so-called new morality of love's license scarcely constitutes the sexual revolution about which we have heard so much. Actually, there is little evidence that our sexual behavior has changed sufficiently in the last few years to be termed a revolution. Freedom is certainly not universal, and tolerance is rarely the rule. In fact, it seems that no matter what attitudes about sexual matters an individual in our society holds, some conflict will result. Even the mass media are becoming sensitive to this situation. Nancy Farber (Look, April 1, 1969,

p. 323) attempts to illustrate this point. She quotes Professor Gary Neubeck, from his course on sexual adjustment at the University of Minnesota (Minneapolis), as describing the conflict in the sexual values of our society:

"Sex is considered both dirty and disgusting and sacred and beautiful."

"We regard sex as something to be treated delicately, but by not talking about it ourselves we encourage those who deal with it grossly."

"We acknowledge the idealism of youth, yet we are afraid to be honest with them about sex."

Karlen (1970) agrees that the so-called sexual revolution is verbally looser than truly sexually free. The actual change in sexual behavior during the last decade seems to be small. Miller and Wilson (1968) found, in a recent questionnaire study of sexual behavior and attitudes, little difference among college students from attitudes expressed and behavior claimed some twenty years earlier. Kinsey and his collaborators (Kinsey, et al., 1953) found a greater sexual revolution in the 1920s than we have any hard evidence for today. Most recent studies (for example, *Playboy* magazine's questionnaire survey published in September 1969) find only scattered and uneven evidence for any marked increase in sexual freedom among today's youth. In view of the recent and rapid increase in the availability of effective contraceptives, what increase there has been seems minimal.

Even if much of today's ballyhooed freedom is illusory, most observers agree that the last few years have seen at least some real upturn in sexual freedom, and particularly in freedom of verbal expression (Luckey and Nass, 1969). In fact, it seems to these writers that what might account for the appearance of great change is that an evolutionary (as opposed to revolutionary) sexual softening has simply passed a threshold for markedly freer verbal expression and communication. Unfortunately, even this process of change seems to exaggerate the conflict in many individuals. The diversity of attitudes in a changing society has apparently not led to a permissiveness concerning differences of belief. Rather, the differences of opinion, fostered by whatever change there has been, seem to have actually increased intolerance of attitudes divergent from our own.

There exists some social punishment (aversive, fear-provoking stimulation) for almost any sexual attitude or behavior manifested in our society. The liberals are labeled "evil," the conservatives "prudish." The net result is that virtually everyone is condemned by some group for his sexual beliefs. The authors suggest that most people would benefit from a generally more accepting and less rigid code of behavior for the entire society.

### The Double Standard

The confusion of sexual attitudes is further complicated by the fact that they are by no means the same for men and women. Similar behavior is received differently depending on which sex acts it out. This double standard, as it is generally called, condemns sexual liberality in women far more strongly than in men. This is not a transitory phenomenon, limited to our culture or age, but rather seems to be almost universally present in widely disparate cultures and throughout most of recorded history. For example, African cultures, both ancient and modern, differing greatly from ours in many ways, display many of the same "double standard" attitudes that we find in the United States today (Akpaffiong, 1970, personal communication). That it exists in modern times in our society is undeniable. Clinical experience emphasizes its pervasiveness and women's liberation movements eloquently describe and condemn it.

So ubiquitous an effect cries for explanation. Before we turn back to a discussion of the effects of the double sexual standard on love, let us see whether we can offer an explanation for its existence. In Chapter IV, we saw that Freud explained the difference in sexual roles by relying heavily on different biologically developed propensities for activity and passivity as well as learning experiences. Here we shall offer an alternative explanation that depends solely on differences in the learning experiences of males and females.

Speculating a bit, let us consider the situation of most male babies and children. It has already been suggested that the mother is the initial love object of the baby. It is usually the case that some male figure does, in fact, compete with the baby for the mother's attention, and compete successfully on many occasions because of his sexual relationship with her. It is easy to imagine that this relationship between "another man" and the male child's primary love object may be very punishing to the child. Later love relationships with females, in which there would necessarily be a significant amount of generalization from the original love experience, would reintroduce the threat and fear of another male's sexual possession of his female. In other words, sexual infidelity on the part of the woman in a love relationship may seem, for the man, a reenactment of the threatening experience of childhood. A woman's situation, however, is different.

For her, mature love involves a relationship with someone of a sex different from her original love object (mother). She has no "traumatic experience" similar to the male child's from which to generalize. Her lover's "outside" sexual activity should not, therefore, be as emotionally upsetting to her as her's would be to him.

This formulation is not intended to condone a double standard (which obviously has many unfair aspects to it) but merely to help explain its existence. Interestingly enough, this hypothesis predicts that lesbians would exhibit more jealousy of their "lovers" than heterosexual women would. According to many clinicians who deal with women in this situation, this is true. Jealousy will be discussed in more detail later. For now let us return to the effects of our confused sexual attitudes on love.

### The Effects of Sex on Love Revisited

As discussed above, the physical aspects of the sexual act are potentially powerful reinforcers, in the development of love. Along with this physically reinforcing effect, emotional, social, and psychological concomitants of sex can be both rewarding and punishing. Sexual acceptance by another human being can be a highly important positive social-psychological reinforcer for those who can respond to it. Consummation of the sexual act (which is often presented as a proof of masculinity or femininity in our culture) can likewise be a strong reinforcer, especially if it has produced pleasure in another human being (the importance of being able to give). On the other hand, guilt, fear of condemnation, or social censure, fear of failure, or fear of loss can all be effectively punishing and can actually introduce a punitive aspect to the interpersonal situation.

The effects of sex on the development of love, then, are indeed complex. These considerations, however, do not exhaust the interrelationship between the two. We now ask, "What effect does love have on sex?"

## Sex with Love

What difference does it make in a sexual encounter whether or not the people are in love?

Remember that our definition of love implies a strong desire to approach, to be close to, or interact with the loved object. Certainly, sexual encounter accomplishes this. The satisfaction of this learned need in the intimate relations of sex is highly rewarding. Love can obviously be a powerful emotion. The consummate satisfaction of this important aspect of the motivations in love afforded by the physical and emotional closeness of the sexual act, therefore, is extremely pleasurable. It adds to the physical pleasure of the sex act itself. In addition, inasmuch as we have internalized the belief that love justifies sex, being in love relieves some of the guilt of the sexual encounter. So love can enhance sex by adding the fulfillment of closeness and intimacy needs and relief from the aversive anxiety-guilt reactions.

## More Self-Defeating Attitudes

Earlier, the all too common situation was described wherein an individual, not sufficiently accepting of himself, rejects someone's approach by devaluing the other person. (If he wants me, there must be something wrong with him.) This devaluation, then, strips much of the reinforcing power from that person. This type of response can occur in the sexual realm.

Almost any individual who is reared in our culture is affected to some extent by the remnants of Victorian morality, described above. That is, virtually all of us, whether consciously or not, have at least a little bit of the feeling that sex is bad. Men are also taught that, to prove their attractiveness and virility, they must make sexual conquests. Besides which, of course, sex is sought for all of the physical and psychological reasons already discussed. When he "scores," however—when he finally takes the girl to bed—it may lead to disappointment and a devaluation of her. The girl's often heard and plaintive question of "But what will he think of me?" has some real basis in fact. The possibility that her lover will think less of her is quite real. This experience, like its counterpart, the trap of low self-esteem, can be tragic. The assumptions and attitudes behind it may be irrational, but that hardly makes it less disruptive.

Furthermore, there is an additional damaging effect of this attitude toward sex. Just as the male may devalue the female for "giving in to him" sexually, he may also devalue himself. The resulting conflict of feelings can give him a momentary blush of success followed by a mixture of pride and guilt. If, in fact, the man suffers from strong inferiority feelings, then he will be unable to fully accept his feelings of pride and accomplishment (except at a very superficial level). This leaves him with the guilt and self-devaluation, which only reinforce the negative self-concept he held in the first place. This "vicious circle" is difficult to escape; attitudes are frequently self-fulfilling because we select stimuli that square with them (even if they are sometimes painful) rather than suffer the punishing anxiety of uncertainty. We often choose to cling stubbornly to a consistent set of negative beliefs about ourselves rather than accept conflicting evidence of worth. This is true because inconsistency, and attendant uncertainty, introduces an inability to predict the consequences of our own behavior. Inability to predict raises the possibility of severe unknown punishment with no way to avoid it. As a result, often we'd rather be left with a certain and secure negative self-attitude than an uncertain and insecure contradiction which could lead to greater punishment. Another way to view this phenomenon is to consider the potential danger in suddenly thinking, "Maybe I can do this after all." Thinking this, we might actually attempt the dangerous act and such an effort could result in the punishment that we feared in the first place.

Once again, the point of all this is that the ambivalent and frequently contradictory attitudes about sex in our culture have caused a great deal of personal unhappiness in general, and a serious interference with interpersonal love relationships in particular. This is especially sad considering the potentially beautiful and important role of sex in love and life.

SUGGESTED READING

Ellis, A. *Sex without guilt.* New York: Lyle Stuart, 1958.

Masters, W. H., & Johnson, V. E. *Human sexual responses.* Boston: Little, Brown, 1966.

Of some value but not to be taken too seriously:

Woodward, L. T. *Sophisticated sex techniques in marriage.* New York: Lancer Books, 1967.

A somewhat better manual:

Ellis, A. *The art and science of love.* New York: Bantam Books, 1969.

CHAPTER VII

# Infatuation

SUMMARY

Infatuation is a state of strong sexual attraction to another based mainly on resemblance to an unreal lover fantasy. The origins of this fantasy are found in early love relationships and in cultural influences. Infatuation contrasts with love in that it possesses no learning history of actual reinforcement by the loved person. It is, therefore, more nearly artificial and less stable. The duration and type of relationship, the progressive development of feelings, and in what terms lovers think about each other, can all supply cues to discriminate infatuation from love. We suggest that marriage might be more lasting if a period of approximately a year were recognized by society as a trial basis before finalization.

In all of our discussions so far, the development of love has been described as a process requiring a long history of highly varied reinforcement dependent in some way upon another person. It obviously cannot be an immediate event. And yet people talk about something called "love at first sight." If first sight cannot be a vision of true love, the phrase seems a contradiction. Even so, we cannot ignore the existence of an experience involving such a strong and almost immediate attraction. What can this be?

Many love relationships start with an intensity at the outset that clearly possesses no long history of reinforcement directly involving the couple. This is true even of some relationships that eventually prove lasting. This sudden and intense attraction has stimulated much pleasure, pain, literature, and art. Regardless of whether it can justifiably be termed love or not, it deserves discussion. It also deserves naming. Let us suggest that it is best termed "infatuation."

66

Infatuation, as love, does not spring from an experiential vacuum. It, too, possesses a learning history. The big difference between love and infatuation is that love's learning history built up around the loved individual, while in infatuation, potent learning experiences occurred prior to the interpersonal encounter and then became relevant through generalization from the past into the present. Two important questions present themselves at this point: "What learning experiences in the individual's history are responsible for infatuation; and, in what way do these experiences influence later interpersonal relations?"

### Love's Fantasies: Early Love Objects

We are all beset and blessed by dreams, day and night. Most are about people; many about love. Somewhere behind these dreams or fantasies of love, there hovers an image of the ideal erotic partner. This image may be narrow and specific, in which case it could truly be called an ideal, or it may be rather broad and inclusive. In any case, it represents a kind of composite of people who possess the potential for fulfilling our dreams of an attractive sexual partner. This image, too, is learned, for we are surely not born with it. Let's discover its origin.

Unquestionably, a prime determinant of the content of this fantasy is our original love object. We generalize from the characteristics of the first person who taught us the love relationship and this forms an important part of our picture of the future lover we wish to possess. Freud stressed the strong influence that characteristics of the parent of the opposite sex have on the selection of a future mate. Although this seems reasonable, it is also true that, in the case of both sexes, there is always a heavy element of generalization from the mother (Chapter V). The picture that we form of our hoped-for partner necessarily includes the physical and behavioral traits of the caretaking person who first engendered love. And, of course, this is usually the mother. There are also significant influences (generalizations), however, from other early love objects.

Every reinforcing person in our early lives leaves some mark on our developing concept of the desirable lover. This concept or fantasy is, therefore, seldom a coherent whole; rather, it is fashioned from a conglomeration of attributes representing the characteristics of all the significant and rewarding people of the past. Hardly surprising, these characteristics are often contradictory. This occurs because the fantasy is predominantly nonverbal. It got started before language did. It can be thought of as consisting largely of a group of disconnected images that do not necessarily form a consistent, veridical picture of any human being, or even a potentially possible human being. Unreality often characterizes this image. No human being can actually fit this picture accurately. Infatuation is based heavily on this somewhat confused image and, hence, is always at least partly unrealistic.

In Chapter III, the development of a love affair that started with infatuation was illustrated. Let's now examine this more fully. The importance of the initial perception that the desired person is attractive to other people was emphasized; but the phenomenon is more complicated than that. Initially, of course, the person must be attractive *to us*. The question is, "What governs this attraction?" We suggested earlier that, somehow, this person fits our lover fantasy. We should explain this more fully.

We suggest that much of this immediate attraction is a response to what we see as features shared with our early love objects. In other words, part of this early attraction is based on generalizations from people for whom we had formed a love attachment in the past. This kind of generalization has been called transference. These similarities need not be obvious nor even necessarily conscious. The loved one doesn't have to look like our mothers (or fathers). Perhaps a gesture, a type of body movement, an intonation; perhaps some reminiscent reaction to something we do. Any of these can trigger a positive response. Usually it is the case that we are unaware of the factors or stimuli responsible for the generalization. In fact, it is even possible that too strong a resemblance, one that we readily recognize, could cause us to reject the person. It's too close for comfort. For example, anything that made the earlier person inappropriate as a heterosexual love object could generalize to the present. When the similarity is obvious, this may produce avoidance. The main point here is that, as adults, some part of our first attraction to another human being results from the generalization of feelings about people important to us in the past.

One potential consequence of this type of generalization is that a transfer of inappropriate responses may occur. Men respond to their lovers as they did to their mothers and women can likewise treat their mates as they did their fathers. In learning terms, this indiscriminate transfer of responses from one situation to another one wherein they are inappropriate is sometimes called "negative transfer," or, in this case, negative transference. Many marriages chug along on this type of transference and can continue to do so for long periods of time. This relative stability, however, does not necessarily imply that this is a desirable situation. Inasmuch as we respond as children when we are adults, we are meeting the world inefficiently. A small amount of this regressive transference is probably harmless, but it can be carried to the point of interference with adult responsibilities.

There are other types of inappropriate or negative transference. We may treat a new lover as we did an old one. The responses may not fit the new situation and the relationship will suffer as a consequence. The generalization from past to present love objects has its potential drawbacks.

## Love's Fantasies: Cultural Beauty

Of course, there are other determinants of our immediate reactions to someone. The picture we have of what we want from a lover includes more than just generalizations from the past. The society in which we live, our general culture, and our special group of associates, all contribute quite directly in telling us what is desirable. The mass media shapes our desires. The hero and heroine of movies, plays, television presentations, even written stories, are all presented in such a way as to suggest just what we should covet sexually. It is clearly stated in one way or another that we should be turned on by slender, even-featured, youthful people with white teeth and every hair in place (although this last may be changing).

There is much that is arbitrary in this picture of beauty that a given culture holds dear. There is certainly little correlation between what is considered beauty (either male or female) in any given group and survival advantage to the individual, the culture, or the race. Of course, some of the characteristics of attractiveness are, in fact, advantageous to survival. Lean good health and the absence of deformity, for example, are adaptive characteristics. But what about mouth size, or nose shape, or the sculpturing of a female calf? What about hair color and texture? These and many other physical characteristics are largely irrelevant to evolutionary survival and the selection of a mate on these bases seems absurd on the face of things. Moreover, since these features of beauty vary considerably from one culture to another, it is apparent that they do not represent absolute values.

It is undeniably true, however, that these cultural values, however arbitrary they may in fact be, do significantly influence our tastes. How closely someone resembles this cultural concept of beauty establishes in some measure his value as a sexual goal object. That is, the degree to which someone meets the cultural standards of good looks and general attractiveness is largely the degree to which he becomes a love prize. This match with the cultural norm tells us, at least in part, how attractive the person will be to others and, therefore, how much envy, admiration, and glory his possession will bring us. In other words, people can be status objects, much as cars or jewelry, and how much status we believe someone can bestow upon us through his interest in us is one determinant of whether or not we become infatuated.

This, too, as a sought-for feature of love objects, is a type of generalization. In this case, however, the generalization is less concrete and direct; it is further removed from the original love object. The generalization from earlier love objects is a transfer of responses from one person to another. The generalization from a cultural norm, on the other hand, is the transfer of an approach response from symbols (pictures and descriptions, for example) to a concrete person; obviously a less direct step.

Infatuation, then, is not as much a response to the actual attributes of a person as it is a response to characteristics that are similar to features found in an unrealistic idealized picture. Since infatuation, by definition, occurs rapidly, the characteristics that are perceived as similar to the fantasy must be readily apparent and may, therefore, quite often be superficial. That is, many of these characteristics are the obviously apparent ones such as looks and superficial life styles, quite unimportant in long-term interpersonal relations. To the extent that this is true, infatuation is unstable and short-lived. Of course, some of the immediately perceived qualities of the infatuated person may be more stable and important, such as consideration for others, degree of aggressiveness, intelligence, and so on. To the extent that it is these more stable qualities that govern the initial attraction will the relationship likely be a more lasting one. In other words, some of the attractions of an infatuation are long lasting and, for this reason, responding to a person whom we immediately view as attractive may give us a better than chance likelihood of finding him to be a truly compatible partner. For the most part, however, we react too seriously to these immediate attractions.

## The Importance of Good Looks

In a delightfully clever demonstration of the importance of good looks, Elaine Walster and her colleagues (Walster, Aronson, Abraham, and Rottman, 1966) showed that this was practically the only thing they could measure that predicted whether or not college students wanted to continue seeing each other. The first impression ranking (by a panel of judges) of the physical attractiveness (good looks) of the students predicted continuing interest. Nothing else they investigated (such as intelligence or concordance of interests) seemed to matter very much in whether or not the students tried to see each other again following a blind date.

Contrary to the expectation of the authors, the women in the study seemed to respond to the factor of physical attractiveness about as strongly as did the men. We are somewhat disheartened by this finding, for good looks do not, intuitively at least, seem very important as a basis for meaningful social relationships.

In a later study, Miller and Rivenbark (1970) found that college students admitted that looks were very important to them, not only in dating situations, but in the presumably more permanent relationship of marriage. In this study, males admitted to a slightly greater interest in the physical attractiveness of their partners than females, but the difference was very small. The investigators rather expected that females would at least verbalize a seemingly more sensible basis for choosing a marital partner, but this did not prove to be the case. Looks were almost as important to women as to men.

What does being physically attractive really mean? It is hard to believe that variations in physiognomy can directly affect the quality of a social interaction, but obviously, direct or indirect, it exerts an influence. The same insecurity that provides the motivation for seeking a sexual status symbol undoubtedly contributes to making beauty reinforcing. If we can continue to use our lovers in social situations to prove our adequacy, we shall continue to enjoy that particular source of reinforcement. Each social encounter can demonstrate anew our ability to attract and capture someone attractive. This undoubtedly has a tendency to disappear; to become less effective as a reinforcer. Other people soon learn other ways to judge our adequacy aside from the sexual partner we can put on display. And the fact that we can attract one good-looking person soon fails to prove to us that we are indeed attractive to everyone. And so, the result is that good looks tend to be more important in the beginning than later.

A continuing insistence on this kind of reinforcement can lead to a type of personality ruled by the desire for conquest. This reaction, called "Don Juanism," will be discussed more fully later. The individual who more strongly responds to other, more enduring, traits is more likely to enter into lasting reinforcing relationships that will develop into mutual love.

The conclusion that good looks can be a source of reinforcement and, perhaps, to some lesser extent, even continuing reinforcement, is hardly surprising. We believe that the prime reason that we respond so strongly to superficial characteristics, such as looks, is because they are easy to discriminate and respond to, not because we have learned through past experience the real importance of these characteristics. More lastingly important characteristics are much more difficult to discriminate "on sight." The conclusion is not unexpected: casual acquaintance, no matter how attractive the other person, is an insufficient basis for committing ourselves to a permanent relationship.

Unfortunately, casual acquaintance, even with one we see often, is the easiest relationship to establish in our culture. Society contributes to the unrealistic aspects of a social relationship by making it difficult for us to learn much about each other. In a social interaction, especially early, custom dictates our behavior to the extent that much of what we do consists of a formalized ritual that reveals little about ourselves that is individualistic or unique. We are expected to approach each other in a relatively well-defined manner; the male making most of the advances and the female accepting only a portion of them. Often the very words exchanged are almost necessarily trite. Some behaviors are required, some expected, and some forbidden. Even among the optional actions, custom hands us a ready list of choices. What shall we do tonight? Watch television? Go to a show? Go bowling?

Social amenities provide us with easy responses to many situations. We know when to visit, when to inquire about health, weather, or relatives. We know when it is appropriate to suggest TV, tennis, or a hamburger. And, indeed, much of this is good. A striking disadvantage, however, is that it makes it more difficult to learn the important aspects of behavior that make people meaningfully different from each other and provide the real substance for individual choices of partners.

## Love and Infatuation

Both love and infatuation represent intense approach responses of one human being toward another. Sexual desire, tenderness, protectiveness, longing, and pleasure are all involved. The similarities are apparent, real, and important. The differences between love and infatuation that we have been describing are, however, also meaningful and profound. The histories are different, some of the associated behaviors are dissimilar and, most important of all, the long-term results are quite different.

The long history of reinforcing interaction between two people provides the ground for a reliable prediction of how the interaction will continue. It is a truism in psychology that past actions are the best predictors of future behavior. Since infatuation is based on superficial responses to a largely unrealistic ideal, it yields little basis for predicting future compatibility. So much for the obvious. The important question now is, "How can we tell the difference between love and infatuation?" Or in other words, "How do we know when to trust our amorous feelings?"

One quite simple but important way is to consider the length of the relationship. What constitutes sufficient time for love to develop is clearly determined by the amount and the variety of interaction. Time alone, however important, is obviously a poor predictor. Association with someone every day during an extended vacation is quite different from being with someone through a variety of daily activities and events. During the course of a year, one may have a year's varied experience, or a month's experience twelve times. The wider the range of experiences two people have together, the more quickly and fully will the relationship between them develop. In addition, the closer their early shared experiences are to the kinds of stimuli and situations they will encounter during the normal course of their lives, the better they can anticipate how they will get along with each other later.

We hesitate to suggest a minimum length of time for the development of love, for we have only intuition and clinical data to go on. Any figure we mention must, therefore, be somewhat arbitrary. But even under the most ideal of circumstances, with the widest variety of shared experience, it seems to us that six months of close relationship might be a bare minimum to serve as a foundation for love. These considerations alone, however, are not enough. The length and variety of interaction are not the only yardsticks by which we can measure love as opposed to infatuation. There are additional cues that come from our behavior and feelings themselves.

Recall that we are motivated to believe that the potential lover really matches an ideal. Since we have little actual experience on which to base this ideal, it is apparent that we must engage in a great deal of active imagining. The less we really know about someone, the easier it is to believe that he has the attributes and behaviors that we want him to have. This implies that we spend a great deal of time in imagining our potential lover in situations which have not, in fact, occurred. On the other hand, if we have shared many real experiences with a person, it is more difficult to attribute fancied behavior to him. Rather, it is easier to recall pleasant moments from the past. Therefore, another way to judge the proportion of infatuation as opposed to that of love is the relative amount of time spent in fantasy over purely imaginary events versus the time spent in happy recollection of actual past encounters. Or, perhaps the latter may be used as a basis for imagining similar experiences that could occur in the future. These memories may not all be perfect; nevertheless, they are real.

Since increasing knowledge about a lover decreases his ambiguity as a stimulus and, therefore, our ability to make up fantasies about him, increasing knowledge should weaken infatuation. Obviously, this may or may not lead to love. If, as the affair is progressing, the feelings of attraction grow less intense, then the relationship must be based heavily on infatuation. The opposite is true of love. Longer interaction should increase the desire to approach, the feeling of closeness in sharing, and, of course, affection. So, taking into consideration the fact that all relationships fluctuate to some extent, and that moods and motivations vary from day to day, an additional cue as to whether or not we are in love is the general direction in which our feelings are changing.

If there is one clear conclusion that we can draw here, it is that time together (under a wide variety of circumstances) is an absolute requirement for predicting a lasting relationship. The more nearly the shared experiences resemble those likely in the future, the better the prediction. Marriages would undoubtedly survive more often if people lived together under realistic circumstances before they pledged a permanent union. Today, many young people are doing exactly this by living together before marriage.

The disadvantages of "premarital marriage" in a society that is ostensibly geared to other arrangements could destroy many of the benefits by making the situation both artificial and anxiety-ridden. The couple is living together under forbidden and, therefore, romantic circumstances. Much of their experience cannot be generalized to the more widely accepted and formalized marital state. Anxiety may hinder the relationship by adding stress. On the other hand, such a union might even strengthen the feeling of closeness by making the two people "allies against the world." In any case, it is probably not the ideal test. A formal arrangement whereby marriage contracts become final only after a year of cohabitation, or in the event of pregnancy, might be a better answer in our society. This year would afford good opportunity as a test of love—and an opportunity for it to develop further if possible. This arrangement, a so-called "trial marriage," has been proposed by many social thinkers, from Bertrand Russell to Margaret Mead.

SUGGESTED READING

Aronson, E. Some antecedents of personal attraction. In W. J. Arnold and D. Levine (Eds.), *Nebraska symposium on motivation*. Vol. XVII. Lincoln, Nebraska: University of Nebraska Press, 1969.

Bersheid, E., & Walster, E. *Interpersonal attraction*. Reading, Massachusetts: Addison-Wesley, 1969.

# CHAPTER VIII

# Frustration and Conflict; Love's Dilemmas

## SUMMARY

When our approach or escape responses are blocked, we suffer frustration and mounting tension. In modern society, this is most likely to occur in the realm of personal and social striving, and especially in the situation we call conflict. In conflict, we are caught between equal and opposing alternatives. We are blocked in the fulfillment of needs because we are unable to move effectively in either direction. The chapter analyzes conflict and conflict resolution in some detail.

The effect of frustration is to raise the level of tension. This either brings about a constructive attack on the "obstacle" or leads to a destructive and self-defeating outcome. Practical suggestions on how to resolve frustration and conflict are offered.

Irrational emotions can interfere with problem solving and lead to abnormal behaviors. Love and sex are rife with illogical fears and anxieties. If frustration of a drive is complete and long term, we extinguish our attempts to satisfy it. If the frustration is long enough, broad enough, and severe enough, it can lead to apathy.

Here and there, and especially in Chapters V (Early Reinforcing Interactions) and VI (Love and Sex), we have mentioned "frustration" and "conflict" without offering explanation of these terms. Implicitly, we have begged the reader's indulgence, called upon his intuitive grasp of these notions, and moved along. It is time to come to grips with these important concepts. In the broad spectrum of human experience, frustration and conflict play major roles. They more or less dominate the arena of love.

76

Frustration arises when circumstances prevent us from fulfilling a need or drive; in other words, when our approach or escape responses are blocked. If hungry, thirsty, or sexy, the absence of food, water, or an appropriate sex object frustrates us, *especially if we have come to expect their ready availability.* We experience discomfort and stress. For most of us, infancy is the only time our biological needs may be frustrated. Our economy of plenty affords the vast majority of middle-class America ready access to all the primary reinforcers, save one. Food, water, and shelter, for example, are all usually available. It is only in the event of natural catastrophe such as flood, storm, or earthquake that we suffer frustration of the primary drives. The exception, of course, is sex. Regulation, and therefore, frustration, of sex is built into our society. When we turn from the biological to the social and personal needs, however, the story is quite a different one. Frustration is a common experience with all of us as we seek to express our learned needs and drives. We frequently experience the blocking of approach and escape responses as they relate to personal ambition and/or desired social interaction with others.

The young girl who sits teary-eyed before the silent telephone during the week preceding the Junior-Senior prom is certainly frustrated. But it is not her biological drives that suffer the most. She is blocked in the fulfillment of her social expectations. The young man who fails to attract a girl, any girl, who is constantly rejected for one reason or another, suffers severe frustration. Although, of course, this constitutes a block to his sex drive, it is of equal importance (probably greater) that this represents to him a failure to carry off what he believes to be the role his peers expect of him. He is as much a social or personal failure as a frustrated biological organism. Perhaps more so.

The bride whose honeymoon fails to yield her immediate and frequent orgasm may be frustrated. But, again, it is not her biological needs that suffer the most; she is frustrated mostly in the fulfillment of an expectancy taught her by modern society. She has failed to achieve what her status as an "enlightened woman" not only says she can, but goes so far as to suggest that she should.

We react to frustration in more or less consistent ways; some leading to healthy resolution; some to destructive and self-defeating outcomes. In a moment, we shall examine some of the consequences of frustration, and some of the ways we react to it. But first we should take a look at conflict. It is here that we find quite a common source of frustration, for conflict, like any other barrier, blocks the expression of needs.

### Conflict as a Source of Frustration

When an individual must choose between two equally attractive goals, must decide between two equally repelling alternatives, or when he finds a single goal to be, at the same time, both attractive and repelling, he is in conflict. In this frequent human experience, we find further occasion for frustration. When alternatives balance each other, we cannot "move" in either direction. We are as surely blocked in the fulfillment of our needs as the prisoner surrounded by steel bars. Fable has it that the donkey that found himself equidistant between two bales of hay, starved to death. Conflict can certainly starve us in the midst of plenty, in many ways.

Frustration in the love relationship quite commonly arises out of conflict. And conflict, almost necessarily, is part and parcel of love. In love, alternatives are always many and choice often comes hard. Conflict is the rule, not the exception.

We can become conflicted in several ways. If two alternatives are equally attractive, we suffer what psychologists call an approach-approach conflict. Two equally strong approach responses are simultaneously activated. We desire both outcomes. As a date for the party, will it be Joan or Betty? Both are attractive and socially talented. This is approach-approach conflict, although it is not a serious one. If the choice is between Joan or Betty as a marital partner, or between career and marriage, the conflict can get sweaty. In general, the greater the significance of the alternatives, and the more lasting the commitment, the severer is the conflict.

Approach-approach conflict is usually unstable; that is, two pleasant alternatives rarely tie our hands for long. It is the nature of an attractive goal that it becomes more attractive the nearer we approach it. Psychologists have called this the "goal gradient." Thus, tentative, even accidental, "movement" in the direction of a positive reinforcer usually enhances its strength and weakens the alternative. The conflict is resolved. The two goals are simply no longer equally attractive. The block is removed. But we are talking here about what might be called "pure" approach-approach conflict, something of a rarity and seldom a problem. In truth, it usually happens that approach-approach conflict is really experienced as what is called "double approach-avoidance." To obtain the one goal, the other must be surrendered, and this loss constitutes a highly undesirable outcome; one to be avoided. Joan and Betty may be equally attractive as potential marital partners, but to marry one is to lose the other. Each outcome, then, is at the same time, both attractive and repelling—double approach-avoidance. This type of conflict is usually both severe and difficult to resolve. Indeed, the approach-avoidance conflict may be experienced as the worst of human dilemmas. We shall examine the reasons for this in a moment.

In another situation of conflict, the alternatives may be equally unpleasant or equally repelling. This is called avoidance-avoidance conflict and is illustrated in the dilemma of the youngster who is told that he must eat his spinach or go to his room. But for other considerations, he would do neither, of course. He would simply turn his back on both unpleasant alternatives. But the parents will have none of this. He is compelled to choose one or the other. Threat of even worse punishment holds his feet to the fire. If the taste of spinach and banishment to his room are equally unpleasant prospects, he suffers an avoidance-avoidance conflict.

Avoidance-avoidance is likely to be a more stable or continuing conflict than approach-approach. To move away from an unpleasant alternative weakens its negativity, it is true. But, in so doing, the individual moves closer to the other alternative, increasing its unpleasant character, driving him back in the direction of the first. He is likely to find a position midway and remain locked there. Unfortunately, circumstances usually impose a time limit. He must eventually make a choice.

Avoidance-avoidance is rarely suffered in the love relationship. It is the approach-avoidance conflict that prevails here. Perhaps, in affairs of the heart, this kind of conflict is inescapable. In approach-avoidance, the single goal possesses both positive and negative value. It is attractive, encouraging approach. It is, at the same time, repelling; there are also unpleasant consequences associated with this action. We experience what has been called ambivalence. We want it, but we are scared of it. Simultaneously, we want to approach and avoid. Promise of reward and threat of punishment offset each other and produce immobility. Neither need is met. Both are blocked, for movement in either direction tends to be opposed. It is the nature of avoidance responses that they often appear to have a steeper goal gradient than approach responses. That is, they not only become stronger as the goal is approached but the change in strength is more rapid than with approach drives. Thus one can find himself at a distance from the goal where the positive and negative aspects seem equal; but if he moves toward the goal, the escape tendency increases faster than the approach and he is driven away. If he moves far enough away, the escape motivation diminishes faster than the approach and so he is once again pulled toward the goal.

Approach-avoidance is one of the most painful of all human dilemmas, for we feel the responsibility of decision to be more squarely upon us than in the externally imposed avoidance-avoidance conflict. And it is often quite difficult to resolve. Hamlet's soliloquy is literature's most eloquent instance. Illustrations from the realm of love are legion. To marry or not to marry, to divorce or not to divorce, to accept or reject an adulterous relationship, to have children or remain childless, to confess an affair or remain silent. Each of these actions promises reward and threatens punishment; if these are equally intense, action is blocked. The individual is indecisive, paralyzed and unable to move effectively in either direction. Usually, he vacillates. First he approaches, and then he pulls back. He repeats this behavior again and again but he never approaches too closely the desirable-threatening goal. It is, of course, the desirability or the promise of reward that holds him in the situation and more or less insures continuing conflict.

Some approach-avoidance conflicts come to us, so to speak, ready-made. They are social legacies; attitudes held by many, many people. And they are handed on to others by word and example. The conflictful attitude toward sex described in Chapter VI is a case in point: sex is at the same time beautiful and sacred but also disgusting and dirty —approach-avoidance.

## Effects of Frustration

Whether it arises from the blocking of a biological or primary drive, from interference with the expression of personal and social goal striving, or from the paralysis associated with conflict, frustration serves to arouse the individual; to increase his level of tension. He is stressed. The extent to which tension is raised depends on the intensity of the drives involved and on the strength of the obstacle. The young girl whose status-hungry parents saddle her with the demand of a spectacular marriage, suffers severe tension if her popularity with eligible males is less than sweeping. In the absence of this strong parental pressure, her frustration is far milder. If the bride believes strongly in the Western tradition of romantic marriage (". . . and they lived happily ever after."), she will find the grind of everyday marital living a sharp contradiction. The extent of her disappointment (frustration) and associated tension will be determined almost exclusively by the strength of her conviction that marriage should be an ideal and problem-free state. If this is unshakable, she is in trouble. The young woman who is pushed by sexual and social urges in the direction of premarital sex, and who is at the same time turned away by moral considerations, may become deeply conflicted. The degree of tension suffered in her approach-avoidance conflict may become unbearably high if these two opposing urges are powerful ones.

In our complex society, some frustration is inevitable. All of us suffer what might be called short-term frustration. And this presents few problems. Continued frustration is something else, for the tension associated with chronic frustration tends to mount or accumulate over time. How often are we startled at the suddenness with which some marriage breaks up. "Sure surprised me. I thought they had it all together." Sudden divorce is seldom sudden. Only on the surface. This marriage was, in all probability, a veritable time bomb, with frustration-induced tension mounting until it reached unmanageable proportions. You cannot sweep frustration under the rug or just look the other way.

The immediate effect of increased tension is to generate greater effort to overcome the obstacle, whatever it may be. In the personal or social realm this takes symbolic form. We think and we stew. We consider and reconsider. We reassess and redefine the situation. In so doing, the problem may be seen more clearly as inessential details that cloud the issue are stripped away and fresh considerations enter. This is constructive action; the product of a problem-solving process. Often, lasting values are discovered in this way. What was a short-term curse may turn out to be a long-term blessing.

Let's look at the dilemma of the starry-eyed bride whose marriage falls short of the romantic ideal she expected. In her state of high disappointment, she may, for the first time, get a glimpse of the substantial virtues of marriage. Because she is now looking, and looking hard, she perceives other meaningful values—social mobility, ready help in crisis and need, the prospect of children, relaxed financial stress, shared goals, and a comfortable place in society. In the face of these considerations, her frustration may give way slowly.

What about the young man who fails to attract a girl? In his state of frustration-induced tension, he may finally come to grips with the reasons that defeat him. Self-examination, as an attack on the obstacle, may uncover the personal shortcomings that block his approach responses. Perhaps, if we can believe television commercials, this may turn out to be as simple as bad breath. Or, the reasons may turn out to be as complex as subtle socially irritating attitudes established in his early love relationship with his mother.

We are talking here about manageable, if intense, frustration. Each of us possesses a certain tolerance for frustration; some of us more, some of us less. When this personal threshold is exceeded, tension becomes catastrophic or overwhelming in its intensity. Aggression, withdrawal, or total disorganization results.

Tolerance for frustration is learned (Mowrer, 1960, pp. 468–472). It is a product of experience and common sense tells us that, like physical disease, it must be suffered in mild doses before resistance can be built up. We believe that child-rearing manuals urging total permissiveness in the management of youngsters preach education for unreality. Better the child experience some early mild frustration (discipline). This will build in him the capacity to withstand the more severe frustrations of adulthood that will inevitably come his way.

*Conflict Resolution*

When frustration arises out of conflict, it will persist, of course, until the conflict is resolved. How, then, are conflicts settled? Quite obviously, perhaps, conflict will disappear only when one or the other of the two equal but opposing responses gains dominance. Either the one must weaken or the other must gain strength, for it is the condition of equality that sustains the conflict and blocks "movement."

In the instance of approach-avoidance (and, again, this is a very serious type of conflict), approach will come about either when the goal becomes more desirable or when its threatening aspects diminish. Alternatively, resolution may come in the form of movement away from the goal (avoidance) if either its negative character is augmented or its desirability is weakened. The paralyzing balance is upset by a change in motivation. The young woman in conflict over premarital sex will move in that direction (approach) if the sexual and social urges grow stronger for any reason. She will also move in that direction if the moral considerations that check her weaken. Reverse these motivational shifts and she will move away; her conflict is resolved in favor of avoidance. And she can be equally comfortable with that alternative.

What brings about these motivational shifts? What could happen that might increase the desirability of the goal or weaken its threatening character? Time and happenstance are factors, of course, but not ones to be counted on. If, unexpectedly, another attractive man should enter the life of this conflicted young woman, her conflict may be resolved in favor of movement away from her lover. This comes about not because premarital sex with him is now more threatening, but because its appeal is diluted by a new attraction. Sometimes conflict is resolved that way. Unexpected events drastically change the situation. More often, however, resolution comes about through the same process that eliminates any other obstacle to need fulfillment—through assessment, reassessment, and a redefining of the situation; in other words, through problem solving. Other values are searched and alternatives weighed. In the process, something may be discovered that tips the scales one way or another. The young woman may enter into premarital sex if the relationship takes on the appearance of "true love." (We talked about this in Chapter VI.) Its appeal is enhanced by this additional consideration. And approach now takes place. Or, she may move away when there is added to its already threatening character, the thought, "He will think less of me if I do." This tips the scales toward avoidance. Temptation is weakened by the addition of more threat.

In laboratory studies, psychologists have discovered a number of factors that help or hinder problem solving. Observations of children and adults engaged in solving abstract problems (puzzles, also mathematical and other reasoning problems) have suggested some rules that determine the ease or difficulty with which we solve problems. We believe that these rules can be applied to the personal realm; that they may aid in resolving frustration and conflict. There is a strong "structural" resemblance between the laboratory puzzle and the personal puzzle (especially when the latter can be viewed objectively). We do not claim that these rules will solve all personal problems. We do claim that they will *help* in formulating a strategy for attacking obstacles to the fulfillment of personal and social needs. And in the resolution of conflict.

*Practical Guide to Frustration and Conflict Resolution*

1. Spell out the problem in detail. Then strip away those details that are inessential or irrelevant. In other words, reduce the problem to bare bones. Irrelevant and inessential details produce what one psychologist has called "mental dazzle" (Katz, 1950). We could as well speak of "mental clutter," for surplus detail prevents us from focusing clearly on the obstacle and on the true nature of what we really want.

2. Attack vagueness. Try to translate feelings and labels into concrete events. Feelings and labels are often fuzzy yet compelling. We act on them (or feel that we should). Why is something "bad" or "good"—concretely? What are we really scared of—concretely? What does it mean when a particular course of action is labeled "wrong" or "immoral"—concretely? And where did the attitude or label come from in the first place? Did we accept it because someone else said it was so, or did we discover it to be true in our own experience? What at best could happen to us—concretely? What, at worst—concretely? When translated into practical consequences, the problem may shrink or disappear altogether. Or, it may turn out to be a smokescreen. The true source of frustration lies elsewhere.

3. Explore the unusual possibility. Rearrange events temporally. What would the problem look like if the events occurred in a different order; if one thing should happen first rather than another. When faced with a problem, we have a tendency to first apply solutions that have been successful in the past. If these don't work in the present situation, they can get in the way. Old habits often interfere with the discovery of new solutions. Any strategy that gets us "out of the rut" will help.

4. Talk it over with a friend. There are several advantages to this. Problems are seen more clearly when verbalized. As opposed to just thinking about it, talking about it seems to put it "out there" before us. Then, too, a sympathetic ear often serves to relieve some of the pressure. Many problems resist solution because tension is too high. It has been demonstrated in the laboratory that, under duress, problem-solving ability is seriously impaired. Then, of course, the friend may

also contribute relevant information. He may simply know something that we don't.

5.  Take a break. Put the problem aside for a while (if you can). It will probably look a little different when you return to it. During this "vacation," the problem may solve itself, so to speak. Inventors say it often happens that way. The solution to the problem comes suddenly following a period of no conscious effort. This has been called the "incubation" period. Of course, at some level, the individual must be chewing on the problem all along.

6.  Don't act immediately on the first solution if the problem is a serious one and lasting commitments follow. Sometimes a second and better solution will come later. There is a good reason for this. Having discovered one "out," tension is reduced and a second and better solution comes more readily with relaxed effort.

Let us illustrate these principles with the fictional case of Sally. Sally is a woman in her middle twenties who has been married for about five years. She is childless, loves her husband, but finds marriage to be something less than the permanent idyllic romance she expected. To bolster her sagging ego, she becomes involved sexually and emotionally with an attractive and flamboyant co-worker. They become mutually infatuated and begin to fall in love. Their meetings are exciting and Sally's anticipation of them is almost painfully acute. She begins to resent her husband, seeing him as an obstacle to spending time with her lover. Soon, almost as a pleasant game, she finds herself discussing future plans with her lover. Her marriage deteriorates and her tension rises. She is shortly faced with the choice of divorcing her husband or losing her lover for he, too, feels the stress of the situation. The decision is difficult. She loves them both, and either way she moves, she must lose one of them. She is in a double approach-avoidance conflict. She applies our guide to conflict resolution:

1.  She details the problem. The choice is between husband and lover. The husband is considerate, kind, devoted, a good, intelligent companion, and he enjoys a comfortable income. The lover is handsome, exciting, appears to be in love with her, but seems less considerate. Also, he earns less money. The husband supplies security and comfort; the lover provides excitement and flattery. Either would suffer if she chose the other, but her husband presumably more than

her lover. She also details the difficulties of divorce, the upheaval of the change and the possible effects on other people. Sally decides that the hurt suffered by either person from her loss is not directly relevant for if she chooses unwisely, all three will probably suffer. Similarly, she eliminates any consideration of short-term trouble (such as the divorce and other people's opinions) as really unimportant in the long run. She is then left with a comparison of the two men and her probable future relationship with each of them.

2. She now attacks vagueness. She has been assuming that it was desirable to have a handsome husband. She asks herself concretely and exactly, "Why?" What does a handsome husband provide her with? Status? More enjoyable sex? What are the dangers of a handsome (and possibly sought after) husband? What does a rather ordinary-looking man deprive her of? She decides that, in the long run, being handsome is not particularly important. Similarly, she analyzes all of the attributes she had listed for each man and reevaluates the meaning (to her) of each.

3. She tries to vary her thought processes. She considers what she might have felt like if she had been married to her lover and then met her husband. It occurs to her that his consideration, and his other qualities might have attracted her quite strongly; and, in fact, that part of the excitement of the lover relationship might very well have attended *any* affair.

4. She confides in a friend who knows both men. Her friend tells her that her lover has had several affairs with married women. His stability in the relationship appears doubtful.

5. She takes a break and goes back to her hometown to visit friends and family for awhile, leaving both men behind. The decision to break off with her lover strongly commends itself to her after a couple of weeks away from the scene.

6. Nevertheless, she delays her decision by extending her visit another week. At the end of this time, she is more certain of it than before. She returns home, puts her decision into action, and finds life less tense and her marriage more satisfying.

### Problem Solving and Emotions

The rules of resolution are imperfect, but helpful when we apply them. Of course, even if we possessed an infallible method of problem solving, we would not always use it. At times, we might jump to a solution that later seems irrational and maladaptive. In the vernacular, we might think with our guts (or other portions of our anatomies) rather than with our brains. This can be called emotional, as opposed to rational, behavior. But, what, in fact, is this phenomenon of emotional problem solving? Is it truly separate from the rational process? The answer to this last question is "No," although the existence of some process of emotional interference with a "reasoned" solution is, nevertheless, undeniable.

Emotions are not incompatible with logic. They are phenomena of a different order. Our emotional response to a stimulus is part of our desire to approach or escape that stimulus. Our rational response is a method of implementing this desire. How then, can emotions interfere with rationality?

It has already been pointed out that high levels of tension interfere with problem solving. Fear, anxiety, or any strong emotional response certainly introduces disruptive tension. Then, too, our fears and anxieties are not always valid. They may be responses learned in distorted circumstances, or by unfortunate accident. If we fear masturbation, for example, because we are convinced it has serious deleterious effects on the body, we are suffering from an irrational fear that might cause painful conflict.

Irrational fears and anxieties are found at the heart of neurosis. They are peculiarly common in matters of love and sex; and being basically avoidance reactions, they can destroy the approach responses of a happy love relationship. Often, anxieties are generated by faulty self-perceptions and by distorted belief systems about interpersonal (particularly, sexual) relationships. As a consequence, paralyzing conflict is not a rare accompaniment of love. Sometimes, these conflicts, remaining unresolved, result in behavior which we might term abnormal. Chapter XII explores this in greater detail.

## Severe and Unrelenting Frustration

Frustration cannot always be resolved. Sometimes the obstacle is insuperable and we face long-term or permanent frustration. Assuming that the need which is blocked is not a vital one, and that we can physically survive the consequences of the deprivation, the effects of unrelenting frustration are dependent upon how broad and important an area of our lives is affected. In the instance of severe and unremitting frustration of almost all social and psychological needs (such as that experienced by prisoners in concentration camps), the effect on the individual is indeed profound.

Considering for a moment that the net result of frustration, by definition, is that purposive behavior goes unreinforced, it becomes apparent that we are dealing with extinction. In other words, when faced with severe and unrelenting frustration in a very broad area, we simply learn that nothing we do works, and we soon learn to stop trying. This is precisely what we see as a result of this kind of continuing blockage —apathy; a state in which we try to do little or nothing.

Unrelenting frustration in the area of love is not rare. The poor, misshapen, crippled man, for example, is doomed to permanent frustration of his desire to attract beautiful women. This sort of frustration would certainly eliminate his attempts to satisfy this need. The broader the area of frustration, the greater the degree of extinction. The man who, for one reason or another, is constantly frustrated in his heterosexual approach behavior may withdraw, hermitlike, from all contact with women. Since it is possible for him to express his sex drive in another way, however, he may turn to homosexuality. Indeed, this does occur and we shall explore this in Chapter XIII.

SUGGESTED READING

Krech, D., & Crutchfield, R. S. *Elements of psychology.* New York: Alfred A. Knopf, 1958, pp. 307–322 and Chapter XIV.

Kendler, H. H., & Kendler, T. *Basic psychology: brief edition.* New York: Appleton-Century-Crofts, 1971. Chapter 10.

CHAPTER IX

# Marriage

SUMMARY

Marriage places lovers in a new and potentially problematical situation. The final capture of a sought-for lover can prove anticlimactic. Displaced aggression can cause difficulties because we have become certain that our spouses are captive targets. On the other hand, married couples can become increasingly adept at relieving each other's frustrations and in avoiding becoming merely mutual (or, even worse) one way punching bags.

The marital relationship means a sharing of the aversive as well as the pleasurable elements of living. This can be highly disappointing since the lover is no longer associated exclusively with rewarding events. However, intelligent sharing of problems can frequently reduce their punishing aspects and thus contribute to the general well-being of both partners.

Some of the capacity to socially reward our lovers through praise and approval is necessarily lost after a long-standing relationship; but new and important methods of mutual reinforcement can be learned.

Age of marrying seems to be an important factor in the probable success of a marriage. For most couples, the early or middle twenties is apparently the optimal marriage age. The husband's background, personality, and socioeconomic status are associated with success in marriage. The wife must make the greater adjustment to the marital situation, at least as our culture is presently constituted. Appropriate discussion and resolution of conflicts is important in maintaining a happy marriage.

Adultery is not all bad. It can destroy a marriage by offering a falsely more desirable alternative and because it frequently causes damaging dishonesty. On the other hand, it can benefit the marriage by relieving

89

pressures and by making us less bored with, and more excited by, our mates. However, most couples would find adultery dangerously difficult to use as a device to enhance marital adjustment.

Children are complex creatures who may either help or damage the relationship between two lovers. They can provide a common goal and represent mutual accomplishment. They can also present problems and responsibilities that can be aversive. They are probably most beneficial to an already good relationship and potentially most destructive to a shaky one. It is, therefore, unwise to attempt to use children to cement a crumbling marriage, or to have them too early in a marriage.

Love sometimes leads to marriage and marriage may lead to particular problems for lovers. The trite phrase, "the bonds of matrimony" is descriptive, for marriage is, indeed, an external bond holding two people together. It is a commitment, a guarantee that your lover will not leave at any moment. It increases security and decreases tension. This is not entirely as good as it sounds, however, because for all its additional comfort and security, marriage requires a change in the way lovers respond to each other. Much of the intensity of courtship is a direct result of a yearning, a chase, a pursuit. Before marriage, the fact that we are not quite certain that our lovers will always be available to us no matter how we behave keeps us oriented a bit more toward them. We watch for signs of boredom or irritation and are always relieved when they demonstrate that they still desire us. Then marriage—the tension relaxes, the chase ends. Marriage is the final capture and possession. We no longer pursue that which we already possess. Tension and attention decline. In security, we are oriented less to our lovers. In other words, we can now "take them for granted."

We do not wish to imply that this is entirely bad, for there is obviously much to be said for comfort. And yet, comfort is not intensity; it is something quite different from the romantic perception of yearning and burning with desire that characterized the chase. In its place is the opportunity to experience additional sources of reinforcement, leaving us in the somewhat contradictory situation in which love itself can increase, while the conscious feelings of intense need decrease.

One of the most obvious changes in the relationship occurs because of the expression of displaced aggression. Daily events are sometimes unpleasant. They often lead to frustration and anger. Much of this anger cannot be dispelled easily, and it lingers with us. We cannot express hostility toward our superiors; it is impolite to be aggressive to strangers; and our friends may reject us if we are nasty to them. This inability to express anger makes us feel helpless, adds to the frustration and, as a consequence, increases our aggressive drives. Then we go home. Our mates are there, innocent, but available; loved, but securely possessed. We are bitchy, hostile, and rude. We feel better; they feel worse. As often as not, they are in turn nasty to us. This relative freedom to express aggression against our spouses can, in fact, be of genuine benefit. It can also snowball, of course, and lead to more trouble than it relieves. This type of aggressive behavior does not constitute an open and honest expression of feelings. Rather, it is quite dishonest. The true source of the frustration and anger lies elsewhere. Our mates are displaced targets and, hence, inappropriate objects of aggression.

Must the marital relationship follow this pattern? We shall answer this question with an equivocal "No." Husbands and wives can relieve each other's daily tensions by openly and sympathetically receiving displaced expressions of anger, but they need not become doormats. In other words, we can listen, understand, and console only when the expression of anger is given a direction other than toward us. That is, we can shape our mates' behavior along appropriate lines. The key here is differential reinforcement. We should be available, sympathetic, and comforting when an honest and nonpunitive expression of angry feelings is being conveyed, but unavailable as punching bags when it is unfairly directed toward us. The former behavior will be learned; the latter, extinguished. In this way, a couple can turn a potential marital pitfall into a love-enhancing service.

The legal ties of matrimony can unleash other disruptive behaviors. The fears caused by the uncertainty of courtship can inhibit us in many ways. Nuptial security can free both positive and negative ways of behaving that can both help or hurt the relationship.

During courtship, we probably felt compelled to please our potential mates. This compulsion to please may weaken when the external ties of state and society bind us together. And should we then feel further need to capture others in order to again demonstrate self-worth and attractiveness, we'll experience restraint against doing so. Whereas before marriage the capture was still incomplete and the chase still thrilling, after marriage we can experience the pleasure of pursuit only with someone new and as yet unattained. The extramarital affair is the consequence. Of course, for full satisfaction, capture must again be complete, which means divorce and a new marriage. Thus an endless cycle is possible. Obviously, this occurs infrequently. It is, in fact, the extreme case. Once again, the danger is related to the security and self-esteem of the people involved. If reasserting one's worth is a compelling personal motivation, then we'll seek every opportunity to do so, even at the expense of destroying an established relationship. On the other hand, if, in the marriage, our mates have made us feel more worthwhile by a process of actively and honestly valuing us, then the marital relationship will be most difficult to surrender. The lesson is clear. We must strive to be sensitive to the inferiority feelings that our spouses may have, and to make certain that we are the prime agents in reducing these feelings. The consequent rewards of the relationship will usually prove well worth the effort.

## Change of Mutual Reinforcement

Courtship is fun. Lovers seek out pleasant experiences. Dates are shared recreation. Only rarely does a dating relationship get involved with the problems of normal living. It is because of this that mutual love grows so readily. The partner-lover becomes a sign of pleasure, recreation, relaxation, and escape from the aversive activities of day-to-day living.

Everyday living is not so much fun. Earning a livelihood, obeying laws and mores, maintaining harmonious relationships with significant people, and many other trying experiences, intrude upon our pleasures. A marital partner shares these events as well as the pleasant ones. He is no longer exclusively the signal of pleasure he once was. Consequently, when the honeymoon is over, it is far harder to always maintain the pleasurable expectations to which we have become accustomed in the presence of our lovers. A period of readjustment is inevitable.

We face another damaging, and perhaps inevitable, change in marriage. Aronson and Linder (1965) have demonstrated that if we change someone's opinion of us from bad to good, we find this highly rewarding. We are more strongly attracted to that person than if his opinion had been high from the start. Conversely, we are hurt more, and dislike someone more, if we lose esteem in his eyes, than if he has always felt negatively about us. One way of explaining this is to note that when we are aware of an individual's low opinion of us, we experience unpleasant and anxious feelings. If his opinion then changes to a high one, not only is his now high opinion rewarding but there is also added relief from the unpleasant feelings engendered by his formerly low esteem. Similarly, if we enjoy the very good opinion of someone who subsequently changes his mind and thinks much less of us, then to his now low opinion is added the loss of the pleasant feelings we had because of his original high esteem. Sometimes this means that a long-standing close relationship, wherein each partner holds the other in high esteem, may eventually lead to some loss of the ability of the partners to reinforce each other through approval and praise. It may also lead to a gain in their ability to punish each other through the expression of negative feeling. Aronson and Linder (1965, p. 169) illustrate this point with the following example.

"After 10 years of marriage, if a doting husband compliments his wife on her appearance, it may mean very little to her. She already knows that her husband thinks she's attractive. A sincere compliment from a relative stranger may be much more effective, however, since it constitutes a gain in esteem. On the other hand, if the doting husband (who used to think that his wife was attractive) were to tell his wife that he had decided that she was actually quite ugly, this would cause a great deal of pain since it represents a distinct loss of esteem."

This unfortunate effect is obviously closely related to something we have already discussed. We pointed out that new attractions and new sexual capture are frequently more rewarding than the mere maintenance of a long-standing relationship. However, the implications of this extend beyond the social-sexual realm, for it affects the power each spouse has to reinforce and punish the other in broad ways. On the plus side of the ledger, we can exploit the implications of this to our benefit. Since people are more strongly attracted to us if they rise in our eyes than if we have always expressed a high opinion of them (especially if it was initially based on practically no information), we conclude that lavish (and, particularly, phony) praise at the outset of a relationship is not the best strategy to employ in forming a good relationship. Indeed, if it doesn't scare off your potential partner, a negative beginning may benefit future relationships. Many brusque people, who seem almost rude before we really get to know them well, are the ones we often end up liking the most. Let us return to the implications of these considerations for marriage.

Although a long-standing positive relationship can itself lower the potential for some types of mutual reinforcement, this is not necessarily fatal. Not all marriages end in divorce. In fact, the enforced closeness of two lovers can act to buffer both from the aversive events of life. The better two people know each other, the easier it is for them to help each other. Crucial to this advantage is experience under less than the best of circumstances. The total result can be a happier life for both and a stronger marital bond. But the reality of constant contact under abrasive as well as exhilarating circumstances sacrifices some measure of the unadulterated hopeful expectation of pleasure. Life is not exclusively hopeful, and the sharing of it must reflect this. Perhaps a full realization of this fact is our most important lesson here. There is no such thing as a thornless rose bush. Marriage can't be all good. The disappointments, if great and totally unexpected, could wreck the relationship. But if we are cognizant of it, prepare for it, and do not demand perfection, the marital relationship can continue to grow, especially in the solid sense of improving the lot and life of each partner. Care, of course, should continue to be taken to seek pleasures together. Marriage should not end dating. The grind of life should never be allowed to merely smooth out a rut. At least, we should add an occasional groove. Not all couples survive the tortuous traps of marriage. We do not know what percentage of divorces are attributable to the kinds of changes in the relationship imposed by marriage that we have just described. There are many causes of divorce. We shall discuss these later.

*Sex and Marriage*

Sex within marriage is meaningfully different from sex outside of marriage. The potential rewards of marital sex are great but the practice often falls short of the potential. Couples who have enjoyed an exhilarating and satisfying sexual relationship prior to marriage are frequently disappointed soon after their passion is given legal license. They fail to adjust to the changes in the situation. They do not cash in on the potential advantages afforded by their new freedom. Their sex lives deteriorate. Just what are these dangerous differences? How can ease, comfort, and ready opportunity for sexual relations be potentially so deadly to passion? For answers to these questions, we must examine the nature of an erotic relationship.

An erotic stimulus is one that arouses sexual desire within us. As we live and grow, we learn what situations lead to sexual stimulation, arousal, and satisfaction—and what situations do not. That is, actual sexual contact is an event that reinforces the expectation of sexual arousal to previously neutral stimuli. Learning with sex as the primary reinforcer follows the same principles as other learning. Partial reinforcement enhances resistance to extinction; differential reinforcement produces discrimination, and so forth. So if Sam makes love to Mary at 11:30 every Monday night for 3 years in the same house, the same bedroom, and the same bed, he will certainly become aroused at 11:29 in that bedroom of that particular house upon seeing Mary in that well-used bed. But, if this is the extent of his sex life, other times and places will never be sexually reinforced, and so will eventually lose their power to arouse him. In other words, he will learn to discriminate. He sees Mary often, but only under extremely limited circumstances does she signal sex. Sam's expectation that other stimuli will lead to sexual encounters will weaken. And, hence, his erotic arousal to Mary will grow specific to one hour and place. If this limited lovemaking fully satisfies Sam's sexual needs, it is even possible that he will respond sexually only to this situation and become truly indifferent to other women who are not part of his learned sexual habit pattern. But it is more likely that the loss of excitement will leave him with psychological needs for a more varied romantic diet and drive him to other beds and belles.

Why should marriage so often lead to this sexual staleness? Clearly life is easier and less effortful when we learn stable routines to follow. If there are no unexpected disruptions, it is all too simple to follow the same pattern of waking, working, eating, entertaining, and sleeping, day after day. But if supper, television, sex, and sleep become an inviolable order, boredom may result. Let us develop the example of Sam and Mary a bit further.

After the late news, Mary, manor, and mattress, in combination, will constitute an erotic stimulus for Sam. Unhappily, Mary alone, Mary at any other time, or in any other place, will not. Sam and Mary are not excited (sexually at least) by each other *per se*. Let us contrast this with their premarital behavior.

Sam and Mary dated as teenagers. They became heavily involved.

So much so that the parents took note, and consequently took care to deny them free access to easy and comfortable trysting places. Providently, Sam possessed a car. Improvidently, it was difficult to find protected parking places. Sam's car became the scene of only occasional eager encounter. No time or place could be relied upon and, often, disturbing circumstances interrupted their dalliance and dictated that their yearnings (heightened by anxiety and foreplay) remain unfulfilled. Our couple was not devoid of sympathetic friends, however, and sometimes, unpredictably, a temporary love nest would be made available to them. Because of the irregularity of satisfaction and the frequent arousal, Sam and Mary's sexual motivations were usually strong. Owing to this, and to the challenge and romance of the "game," most of the time that they saw each other, they actively sought some place and means to make love. They sometimes succeeded, frequently in haste, but usually happily. Circumstances dictated that a wide variety of places and times be exploited. All was excitement. Sex and life were erratic and erotic. When in each other's presence, the probability of sexual arousal and the possibility of satisfaction were always present. Each became a strong erotic stimulus for the other.

Examine the learning involved. The only constant cue that was always present when sexual relations (the primary reinforcer) occurred, was the other person. Therefore, the presence of the other person alone was conditioned to sexual arousal and became the erotic stimulus. Note also that the reinforcement was partial and unpredictable, fulfilling the requirement for a tenaciously learned association indeed difficult to extinguish.

Now marriage has changed this. No longer must Mary and Sam seek a variety of love nests. Time is with them, as is house and bed. If now is inconvenient, later is always there. As satisfaction becomes assured and predictable, the once constantly high degree of orientation toward sex diminishes. Routine becomes the rule and the conditions for general arousal weaken. Sam now discriminates between Mary in the morning and Mary at night. The former becomes sexless. The bed and the room soon become an essential part of the arousing stimulus until, finally, Mary herself, unsupported by the other cues, extinguishes as an erotic stimulus. The uncertainty and variety that contributed so much to the earlier erotic relationship have turned into a predictable routine; passion has narrowed to specified limits.

Is this lamentable loss avoidable? Certainly, for marriage affords us the potential freedom and opportunity to enhance eroticism virtually as we choose. Although it is quite probably true that we differ in degree of genetic sex drive endowment, we can surely enjoy whatever amount we have to the full extent that the properly guided use of learning principles will allow.

## The Prophylaxis of Boredom

The stale death of passion just described is common. It is a frequent observation that couples become bored with each other and lose the excitement of courtship days. Perhaps some of this is a consequence of the fact that both partners retain vestiges of the sex-is-dirty attitude discussed in Chapter V, and so limit their marital sexual behavior to narrow expression. In doing so, their anxiety over morality and performance, for example, becomes contained but so do their sex lives. Surely, the price is too great. Anxiety, too, is learned, and therefore can be extinguished. A free, exciting sex life within marriage can be so rewarding as to eventually extinguish anxieties over sexual behavior. The point is that changing the behavior, for whatever reason, will usually change the attitude that was responsible for the behavior. It is *not* true that the attitude must be changed first. So what behavior do we recommend? First and foremost, variety. Variety of time, place, position, method, and mood. Freedom and variety, subjective and objective, with no holds barred.

Let us return to Sam and Mary and buy them a membership in "Ennui Anonymous." We shall prescribe a remedy for their rigidity and boredom. First, we disrupt the routine. When Sam comes home for dinner on Tuesday, he brings a bottle of wine with him. He is also armed with thoughts of seduction. Mary is not yet aware of this plan and the wine surprises her. She is really surprised when Sam reaches under her skirt during the second glass and fondles her in the same way he used to when he was "on the make." The preparation of dinner suffers somewhat during a lovemaking session, but neither of them especially minds the pasty potatoes. In fact, since they did not make love fully before dinner, but stopped at the point of high arousal, they barely taste the food. For dessert, with doors locked, and clothes partly on, they make love on the living room couch. Not particularly comfortable, but at least different from their previous deeply fixed pattern. The wine and whimsy make the late news seem less threatening that night but, far more important than that, Mary can never be sure again that 6:30 P.M. is a sexless hour nor the living room chaise necessarily chaste. And Sam will, perhaps, no longer feel it necessary to digest dinner and drama (video) before thinking about sex.

This is not enough to reestablish a truly erotic relationship, but it's a good start. The goal is to recondition each other as adequate stimuli for signaling the possibility of sexual encounter. Dietetic breakfasts of passion instead of pancakes, surprise lunch visits, the room upstairs at your favorite motel-restaurant after a dinner out, a quick feel in the car, and experimentation with technique, will all help maintain this level of excitement, expectation, and arousal.

Variety of time and place are the keynotes to maintaining the high level of erotic expectation in the presence of your partner. Variety of technique adds another dimension to excitement. It is a long-accepted psychological principle that a change of partners increases sexual performance (Grunt and Young, 1952). Perhaps some of this effect is due to an overly rigid and set routine that develops with one partner. Well-practiced motor behavior of any kind eventually becomes automatic. The certain knowledge of what to do next and what the response will be to our actions leads to responses not only devoid of excitement, but practically devoid of thought. When sexual intercourse becomes as routine as this, we neither look forward to it (we don't have to, it will inexorably follow the same course) nor remember it (it's no different from the other 500 times). Variation changes this picture. An uncertain procedure requires thought and planning (looking forward to) and an unusual event stands out in memory. There are literally dozens of marriage or sex manuals on the market to stimulate the thoughts of the interested couple. A few of these are referenced in the suggested readings of Chapter VI.

## To Marry or Not

In spite of the pitfalls of marriage, our society is clearly geared to it. Married adults are healthier, live longer, and are better adjusted emotionally than their unmarried counterparts (statistics on this abound; see, for example, Tenenbaum, 1968, Chapter 35). How much of this is due to marriage, and how much is due to the fact that maladjusted people experience trouble finding mates is impossible to say, but it really makes little difference. Whether healthier, better-adjusted people are produced by marriage or attracted to it (and selected for it), the fact remains that marriage is a sign of cultural adjustment. There are clearly built-in advantages to paired living. Temporary incapacity of one partner can be tended to by the other without requiring intervention by impersonal agencies. This fact alone reduces hospitalization time for married people as opposed to single ones. Shared labors can be accomplished more efficiently. In short, a good marriage supplies each partner with a readily available source of the all-important human reinforcements.

Even so, many marriages do not succeed in even maintaining themselves, let alone contributing significantly to the welfare of the couple (see Chapter X) and many others limp along in misery. What factors account for good and bad marriages? Can we predict successful mating at all, or is it virtually a chance outcome?

Rubin (1970b) has demonstrated that what people call liking and loving are separate entities. He further presents evidence that while both are important in marriage, love is clearly the more crucial element (Rubin, 1970a). Liking is based on admiration for and predictable reinforcement from the liked person, but since love is based on many shared pleasurable experiences and mutual reinforcement, it is a directed conclusion that the more interests and tastes a couple share, the more they can enjoy from, about, and with each other. Opposites may or may not attract, but there is evidence that this does not form the basis for a growing relationship (Scanzoni, 1968).

All of these considerations bring about some obvious questions. Can we predict anything about probable success in marriage from such things as age, educational attainment, and income level, for example? Or, perhaps, from a disparity between the partners on these points? To some extent we can. However, the answers are not simple, but rather suggest that these factors interact with each other. Let us turn to age first.

## Age of Marriage

Marital success is easier to imagine than define. It is most difficult to measure, indeed much more difficult than it appears on the surface (see, for example, Lively, 1969). Even such obvious measures of marital failure as divorce cannot always be applied validly. If we were interested in examining the relationship between religious preference and success in marriage, for instance, we could not use divorce rates to assess this relationship since divorce, itself, is viewed differently by different religions. Here, the factor we wish to explore in its relationship to marital success contaminates the very measure of success we wish to use. Even such variables as income level and education might influence divorce rates. Similarly, there are problems with almost any measure we may wish to employ. The expression of the couple's own assessment of their marital adjustment is clearly affected by many things other than the state of the marriage alone. Third party judgments can be biased and unreliable. Psychological tests of marital adjustment suffer from validity problems. In addition, of course, we are dealing with several highly complex and interrelated factors. Thus many of the conclusions must be tentative, for they frequently lack true experimental support.

Notwithstanding all of the difficulties, one clear fact emerges. Very young marriages stand a very poor chance of success (Cox, 1968; Barry, 1970). The age of the husband is particularly critical in this respect. According to Glick (1957), males who marry before the age of 18 stand almost three times as great a chance of later divorce than men who marry between the ages of 22 and 24. There are probably many reasons for this. Males who marry very young tend to be immature, even for their ages, are insecure and maladjusted, possess a low level of educational and occupational aspiration, and often consider themselves poor marital risks. Perhaps they overreact to any female who shows interest in them (Cox, 1968). It is not difficult to conclude, then, that with all of the problems that would likely face this young couple, they might find it hard to enjoy a mutually rewarding life together.

Moreover, as we shall explore further in the next chapter, people change in many ways. Teenagers are hardly set in their life styles. A person's emotional needs at 17 are not likely to be the same at 25. In our society, this is particularly true of men. With the completion of education, men's lives change radically. The pressures of earning a living and of meeting the world as an adult are greatly different from the skills and demands of a student. Therefore, what things are reinforcing for a teenager are not necessarily the things that will reinforce even the same individual five or six years later. When needs change, so does the effectiveness of the marital partner as a positive reinforcer.

The situation is slightly different for the female. For her, the biggest change in her life style is usually marriage (Pfeil, 1968). She must make the greater accommodation in the marital situation. Student to homemaker, or professional woman to housewife; even if she maintains her previous role to some extent, our culture usually demands that the responsibility of the home be her new primary identification. It is not surprising, therefore, that research is likely to show that differences in age (or, for that matter, education, background, or prior occupation) of the wife at the time of marriage do not influence marital success particularly. No matter what her age, education, or occupation, marriage presents about the same challenging adjustment for the woman.

The fact that the youthful marriage usually gets into difficulty does not imply that the longer we wait to marry, the better the chance for a good marriage. It is not that simple; the relationship seems to be curvilinear. That is, there may be an optimal age for marriage. Difficulties are associated with being either too young or too old. What age is optimal, however, is clearly different for different people. Waiting until our needs have stabilized and will no longer change drastically may be an excellent idea, but waiting until our life styles become so set that we experience great difficulty in accommodating to the demands of the newly shared life may be disastrous. Once we attain our adult roles, we know how to satisfy our desires. If we are alone, then, of course, we learn to rely on ourselves as the primary instrument to meet these needs. Years of solo living make us quite self-sufficient. Our habits become well established. If we then marry, we must extinguish many of these learned responses, for they will most certainly clash with the demands of marriage. Resentment and conflict will follow. In other words, not only the relief of our physical wants but also our entertainment and pleasure seeking may become conditioned to mechanisms of satisfaction that do not readily accommodate a spouse. The lesson is, then, that if we should choose to marry, we should probably do so after we know what directions our lives are likely to take, but before we become too firmly set in them. This would imply that the longer we prepare for our occupations, the later we should marry. For most people whose lives are rather well determined by their early to middle twenties, then, this would seem to be the optimal time to marry. For the few whose occupational preparation requires significantly longer, then, a few years later is probably recommended. In any case, although the principles may be sound, each individual case differs enough to eliminate hard and fast rules.

While discussing even as simple a factor as the effects of the age of marriage on the probability of success, we have seen that many factors interact. Personality, education, and occupation enter into the relationship. This is also true of other factors we may wish to relate to marriage. Let us examine a few briefly. (An organized review of this research can be found in Barry, 1970. See the suggested readings.)

## Socioeconomic Status

Socioeconomic status is a combined index that includes income, occupation, and education, three variables that are clearly interrelated. We might expect these matters to influence our lives profoundly and thus our adjustment to marriage. Indeed, this expectation is upheld. No matter which of the three variables we look at, we find a positive relationship between increased socioeconomic status and both measured adjustment within marriage and duration of the marriage. The reader may recall striking examples to the contrary; that is, the well-advertised tendency of some of our wealthier citizens to shed partners as in a square dance. We must remember, however, that less prominent people have neither the opportunity nor the wherewithal for such actions—and, most important, less visibility when they do. Returning to the relationship, however, we once again find that the husband's ranking on these variables is the critical one. This is not particularly surprising since the most common situation in our society finds the husband's status the predominant influence on the way in which the family lives and is viewed by others.

Cause and effect are again tangled. High socioeconomic status undoubtedly makes life more rewarding. (If it doesn't, our entire politico-economic system is based on a fallacy.) And so we might expect it to increase the positive relationship between two people who share this life. However, it is unclear how much of the better adjustment is attributable to the high status and how much of the higher station in life results from better adjustment. In any case, we are left with the fact of a positive relationship between high socioeconomic status and happier, more enduring marriages.

## Additional Background Factors Influencing Marriage

Earlier, we stressed similarity of attitudes, backgrounds, and so on, as an important factor in establishing a mutually reinforcing and, therefore, enduring relationship between two people. We wish to re-emphasize this. It has long been known that similarity of backgrounds is almost essential to a good marriage. This is not to say that a marriage between two people of ethnically or economically widely different backgrounds is doomed to failure, but clearly it is handicapped. We all come into marriage with attitudes and expectations and it is reinforcing to us when these are met. People of widely differing backgrounds simply do not validate each other's expectations as well as people of similar backgrounds; nor, do they tend to enjoy the same things.

Recent reviews of the research (such as Barry's, 1970) stress the importance of family background factors in the male. It seems that the happier the childhood of the husband, the closer the relationship to and identification with his father and the more stable and secure he is in his masculine image, the happier will be the marriage. This is apparently true because the stronger these attributes are in him, the more his wife perceives him as fulfilling her expectations of a good husband. Furthermore, happily married women perceive their husbands as being rather dominant, clearly a cultural expectation of the male role. Supporting our earlier statement that it is the wife who must change more in marriage, Barry also reports research that indicates that in happy marriages the wife's personality tends to become more like her husband's. In unhappy marriages, on the other hand, the husband's personality changes so that it resembles his wife's less than when he married her. The burden within the marriage, in our culture, is for the wife to make the greater adjustment. If her husband does not meet her expectations, however, she finds it difficult to do so. The wife who enters marriage hell-bent on changing her husband usually fails.

## Conflict

Marriage is bound to see some conflict, hassles, hostility, and aggression. We have looked at conflict, both within individuals and between them (Chapter VIII). Conflict must be satisfactorily resolved and aggression coped with or the marriage will be destroyed by this highly aversive element. Symbolic resolution is often the most satisfactory and sometimes the only means of coping with a frustrating situation. Marriage is no different from the rest of life in this respect, except that frequently conflict cannot be as easily escaped.

Although there seems to be surprisingly little research evidence to confirm this, we believe that married couples who solve their differences through discussion (which is, after all, an important form of symbolic behavior) will suffer far fewer aversive consequences of conflict than those who try to ignore interpersonal conflicts within themselves. It is important to note here that honest discussion is *not* nagging or arguing. As pointed out in Chapter III, these are dishonest manipulations. Aggression and hostility do not simply dissipate if ignored but, instead, fester, causing anxiety and escape behavior. Avoiding topics of conversation, behaviors, and ultimately each other, are the consequence of unresolved conflict. And they contribute to the extinction of love and the destruction of marriage.

## Children

The basic purpose of marriage as a cultural institution is to provide a stable structure for the rearing of children. Whether or not marriage is the best machinery for this purpose is not our concern here. Our principal interest is in the effects children exert on the marital relationship.

Children possess many meanings for parents. They can represent symbolic immortality, biological potency, cultural stability, or they may simply be dependent human beings to be loved and loved by. They can also represent unwanted responsibilities or serve to remind one of mistakes, and they can be sources of frequent irritation.

There is no evidence in humans for a biological need to bear and rear children. We assume, therefore, that it is learned motivation we speak of here. Some of this we probably learned as children when forming attitudes about future social roles. Perhaps much of it was learned later. In any event, many couples want children apparently only because our culture clearly communicates to them that it is only "right and natural" for them to do so. Others desire children for the very real reinforcement they can provide. Children love us, and it is satisfying to be loved. Children need us, and it is satisfying to be needed. Often, children provide a couple with a built-in source of pride and pleasure. Parents can see in their offspring some palpable result of their cooperative mutual effort. They are rewarded by the success of their work together, committed to the continued responsibilities of this work and, thus, are bound more closely to each other. These enhancing effects, however, are largely dependent on the initial strength of the relationship and the security of the couple in themselves and in each other. Insecure people will tend to be more critical and less pleased with their children than those with high self-esteem and security. They will be less able to give and accept the child's love. In other words, unhappily, the reinforcing potential of parenthood is probably the least for those who need it the most.

There is certainly no question that many of the duties and responsibilities of parenthood are aversive. Children are an economic drain and an anchor on the range of activities and entertainments that the encumbered couple can pursue. Two people who are not mutually enhancing, who are not cooperating smoothly and enjoyably with each other, are likely to find the tribulations of parenthood to be punishing and divisive. It is possible for children to provide missing mutual goals and activities, but they can also deepen a rut if it is already present. They can further tighten a routine that is already strangling a marriage. Christenson (1968) notes that the number and spacing of children were not nearly as important to the success of the marriage as was the correspondence between the number of children and the stated *desired* number. Apparently, children are not helpful to the relationship unless the couple wants them in the first place. A poor relationship may simply find children an additional source of irritation. In short, a baby is rarely a cure for a bad marriage.

Thus, as is true of most other complicated affairs, children are a mixed blessing in a marriage. Optimally, they can be enhancing and fulfilling, adding to the couple's enjoyment of life and each other. They can bring parents closer together by giving them mutual goals and shared rewards. On the other hand, the inevitable problems of parenthood can add to the abrasiveness of life and tend to drive some couples further apart. The better the marriage in the first place, the greater the capacity of the couple to enjoy the benefits and tolerate the frustrations of parenthood. It is undoubtedly wise in many ways for a couple to put off having children until their marital relationship is happy, secure, cooperative, and mutually enhancing. Children may help strengthen these things, but they will probably never bring them about.

## Infidelity

Sexual infidelity is not rare in marriage. As a matter of fact, it is common enough that some physicians have well-established routines for treating adulterously contracted venereal disease in both partners while concealing the true nature of the disorder from the innocent party. The dangers of adultery have been well advertised and need not be elaborated here, but a few words concerning the problem seem appropriate.

Adultery usually means dishonesty. By dishonesty, we mean cheating, outside sexual contacts that are hidden from the spouse. Some dishonesty is almost inevitable. Some women and most men are terribly threatened by someone else's temporary sexual possession of their partner (see Chapter VI). Our culture stresses exclusive possession in intimate relationships and there are several aspects of an adulterous relationship that can be threatening to a spouse. The dishonesty and dissimulation that can result from simply trying to hide these potentially painful truths from our mates can bring about the avoidance behaviors that we have previously found destructive of love. Further, it cannot be denied that some adulterous relationships become rewarding enough to pose the threat of actually replacing the marriage. Often the second relationship is falsely more desirable. At the time, it is initially inviting for all of the reasons presented earlier in this chapter, the thrill of the chase, for example.

Adultery can exert a beneficial effect on a marriage. Couples who are quite secure with each other and not unduly threatened by potential loss of each other sometimes find that an occasional outside relationship actually enhances the marriage. No person can always be everything to his mate. Another relationship may take some demands off the marriage and allow it to relax somewhat. And because variety is sexually stimulating, affairs need not drain away sexual pleasure from the marriage. Moreover, since we may find it difficult to continue indefinitely to value our mates as desirable sexual beings, the demonstration provided by adultery, that our spouses are indeed attractive to others, can be of benefit. Even the marital insecurity brought on by an amorous affair is not totally detrimental. It may counteract the dangers of "taking for granted" that we described earlier. Unfortunately, however, it is probably the case that those who would feel the greatest need for the excitement of adultery would likely be those who valued themselves (and thus their partners) least. Hence, being insecure in the first place, they would tend to be most easily threatened by the affairs of their mates. They suffer an avoidance-avoidance conflict between the Scylla of Boredom and the Charybdis of Jealousy. All things considered, however, there are many circumstances where sexual variety for both marital partners may be exciting and stimulating to their own relationship. Long lost lusts can be awakened, new techniques learned, new respect generated, and constricted appetites newly expanded.

We must emphasize, however, that the dishonesty that usually accompanies an affair is almost impossible to avoid and is potentially highly destructive. Adultery is a serious matter. An unusually good knowledge of ourselves, our spouses, and our marriages is required to avert disaster. We must, for example, be fully able to avoid feeling guilt about ourselves. We must also be free of moral indignation about our spouses. It is probably true that most couples in our society would find that the destructive aspects of adultery outweigh its benefits, at least as far as the marital relationship itself is concerned. We are merely pointing out that infidelity is not always and inevitably bad.

SUGGESTED READING

Barry, W. A. Marriage research and conflict: an integrative review. *Psychological Bulletin*, 1970, 73, 41–54.

Landis, P. H. *Making the most of marriage* (4th edition), New York: Appleton-Century-Crofts, 1970.

Russell, B. *Marriage and morals.* New York: Bantam Books, 1966.

# CHAPTER X

# Loss of Love

SUMMARY

Love, even when well established, may extinguish. It seems likely that close to fifty percent of all marriages end in divorce or separation. Although some of these may be due to the fact that the couple were never really in love in the first place, the fact that the median length of a divorced marriage is about seven years argues against this as the principal explanation.

People change as they grow older. Needs and life styles are partly a function of age, and so motivations and behaviors change as we mature. Since couples do not always change in the same direction, they may come to please each other less and need each other less. The maturing needs of men, particularly, tend to be less oriented to their marital partners than they were during courtship. The physical deteriorations of aging, although, in reality, affecting men sooner than women, are viewed in our culture as decreasing the physical attractiveness (and, therefore, reward value) of women first.

Divorces rarely seem to lead to a disenchantment with marriage. Divorced people are highly likely to find new mates, usually within the first five years following the divorce.

The repetition of most, perhaps all, human activities may ultimately bring on a sense of monotony or boredom and the impulse to turn to some other pursuit. The implication that the love relationship must eventually weaken because of this principle is rejected.

People change, and thus, also, can love. Time transforms needs and circumstances change behavior. Our lovers meet our needs and, in turn, we behave to please them. But neither these needs nor the behaviors are static. They change as we live. Lovers can change together, and although neither remains the same person the other learned to love originally, the relationship may continue as strong or stronger than at the outset. It is more often the case, however, that lovers grow apart and love extinguishes. They then separate or share a loveless life.

How often does a close love relationship dissolve, for one reason or another? Divorce rates, at best, provide only a partial answer, for many love relationships are never formalized by marriage. And so the "divorce" doesn't show in the statistical record. The statistical record, incomplete as it is, is gloomy enough. In 1928, there was approximately one divorce for every 12 marriages (Landis, 1970). In 1948, the ratio was about one divorce for every 2.5 marriages (Rutledge, 1966, p. 236). In 1969, about one for every 3.2 marriages (USDHEW, 1970). It would appear, then, that the big surge in divorce rate occurred between 1928 and 1948, and that for the past twenty years, it has more or less stabilized at approximately one divorce for every three marriages.

The statistical record is more likely a reflection of changing social views about divorce than a realistic representation of the number of failing marriages. Adding to the bleak picture of high divorce rate is the fact of a growing incidence of "informal divorce," separation without benefit of court action. Indeed, the number of married couples who maintain separate residences may be actually greater today than the number who obtain a legal divorce. And few of these seem to result from compelling employment or service commitments.

Rutledge (1966, p. 237) estimates that over fifty percent of people who marry eventually separate. Although some of this occurs because of too-early marriage (infatuation rather than love), most cannot be so explained. The median duration of marriages that end in divorce is 7.2 years (Rutledge, 1966), while the mode, or peak time, falls in the third year (Landis, 1970). This is obviously more than enough time to have discovered that the compelling force for the union was infatuation rather than love. Either considerable time is required to fall out of love, or the marriage holds together for a while as a loveless union.

Further, many people whose mutual love has long extinguished, often continue to live together. So the problem is hardly inconsequential. Loss of love, extinction of approach behavior, dissolution of the relationship—however, you wish to label it—is pervasive and begs for understanding. Let us try to understand it.

*Changing Behavior*

We grow, mature, and learn; therefore, we change. We must learn to act differently in order to meet new problems and to simply continue to respond appropriately to our environments. The behavior of a 20-year-old is not generally acceptable when we (and our friends) are 35. The carefree attitudes of youth become the irresponsible actions of the family man. Responsibilities dictate behaviors, and age and circumstances modify abilities and inclinations.

A love relationship is established on the basis of mutually reinforcing behaviors. Once well established, love is difficult to extinguish. The generalized and unpredictable nature of the reinforcements builds in a high resistance to extinction. But people will eventually give up approaching a stimulus that has essentially ceased being reinforcing—if it has been nonreinforcing long enough. That is, if two lovers change in such a way that they please each other only infrequently or not at all, love will die.

We cannot truly separate changes in behavior from changes in motivation. Such a division is completely artificial, since the concept of motivation is a means of trying to explain behavior. Therefore, it is meaningless to talk about one and not the other. But, for the sake of convenience, we shall partially effect such a division. We shall view the effects of the changing behavior of one lover on the love responses of the other, and the influence of one's changing needs on his own love for his mate.

Chapter IX dealt extensively with marriage and its effects on the couple; consequently, their relationship. It was pointed out that the mere fact of living together in daily contact, and the security of the marital contract, can create a situation in which the couple no longer reward each other as often as before. This was attributed directly to the change in their responses to each other and the fact that they were together during times of duress as well as pleasure. When the couple shares a traumatic event, such as the death of a loved one or a severe financial setback, they may be brought closer together. But the constant abrasiveness of daily difficulties undoubtedly tends strongly to drive them apart. It is interesting to note, with respect to this, that there are approximately three times as many marital breakups in nonwhite U.S. citizens than in whites (Landis, 1970). Is this a result of the far more aversive socioeconomic milieu suffered by the nonwhites, leading the couple to falsely associate with each other these severely punishing daily events? Perhaps.

However, in addition to the effects of marriage, behavior changes as a function of merely growing older. There are obvious manifestations of this. The woman who was captivated by the prowess and fame of a professional football player will find that this image rarely continues into the middle years. The man who marries Miss Teenage America will soon discover her youthful beauty is a fleeting thing. But far more general than this, there are changes. A young pair, newly coupled, can maintain for a while the free behavior of youth. During adolescence and young adulthood we are usually actively engaged in seeking wide experience. We test our planet, powers, and pleasures. We gather information on latitude and limits. And so, we learn what we like best, what we do best, and what we fail at. Thus, we narrow our activities. We concentrate on the behaviors for which we were most frequently reinforced and settle into a routine that affords us satisfaction. We grow up, which is partly to say that we grow narrower.

At the same time, other things are happening to us. The involvements of the husband and wife with each other grows progressively less. Our roles differentiate and diverge from each other (Blood and Wolfe, 1960). For many of us, as we move from youth toward middle age, our jobs become more complex and demanding; professional responsibility grows. The net result is that our vocations take up more of our time and energy. This is exaggerated by the likelihood that we have changed our style of living in such a way as to increase our financial obligations. Children and suburban houses cost more than pet cats and one-bedroom apartments. They also demand more time. So we find ourselves spending more time and, hence, a greater proportion of our activities, in our jobs and in merely maintaining the trappings of our life styles. Even if it is not a demanding job, other activities increase. Something must be sacrificed. It is difficult to make love while cutting the lawn; it is impossible to see a nightclub show while changing a diaper or emptying the washing machine. Leaving the house becomes a strain. Television replaces concerts, movies, evenings out, and even vacations. In effect, less attention is now paid to a wide variety of mutual enjoyments and, ultimately, even to each other. Of course, the rigid routine makes it easier to meet the increasing demands on our time. It also makes it easier to fall into a too-narrow, too-confined, and too-fixed pattern. The very behaviors that we admired, enjoyed, and came to love in our mates may be the first ones to go. Carefree, anxiety-free, shared pleasures, and times of happy surprise are the most vulnerable behaviors to the axe of responsibility. As our lives become routine and predictable, we become automatons, and automatons don't love, nor are they very lovable. It becomes increasingly important to break routine as a planned thing. And, if the couple wishes to protect their mutual love, it becomes necessary to sometimes break the routine together.

Earlier, we indicated that there was another side to this coin—that changes in needs could be part of the explanation of changing behavior and part of the reason we might grow away from our lovers. Let's look at this now.

### Changing Needs

As long as we live, we shall require food, water, sleep, and shelter. We shall also require some amount of stimulation and exercise, along with some sort of sexual outlet, social contact, and personal success.

The first of these, the elemental biologically vital needs, will change in only minor ways as we grow from youth to old age. We may eat a little less and sleep a little more after we pass the middle years but, by and large, the behaviors we learned in youth to satisfy these needs will serve us without major change until age makes us too feeble to utilize them. Not so for our social and psychological needs. A teenager is a pretty much undifferentiated human being. No one is quite sure what path his life will follow. He might saw wood or bones; he might become a justice or a jailbird. The activities that seem most important to him in his prevocational age are generally those having to do with the acquisition of social skills. And social reinforcements are terribly potent. Most people this age are not required to earn a living. They are rarely concerned with their future lives, and usually only passingly interested in matters of family responsibility. The principal passions are acceptance, approval, and the attainment of love from peers and parents. How easy it is at this age to become infatuated with, and even learn to love, someone who can satisfy these social needs. But later, will the same person continue to be reinforcing to the same extent?

Later, other motivations become prepotent, and other reinforcements are sought. The need for social success is partly displaced by the need for vocational success. Concerns about adolescent attractiveness subtly change to worries about health and wealth. The new responsibilities of job and family require new behaviors. The earlier ability of a lover to reward by lowering his partner's youthful anxieties is no longer adequate. It must change to meet the new needs. Man or woman, what we want and need at 30 is different from our requirements at 20.

Many of these changes automatically affect a couple's relationship. A man's activities during his productive years become increasingly centered on matters outside the home. A woman's concern with her husband becomes diluted with her concerns for her children and tangential domestic issues; sometimes with an outside job. All in all, it becomes increasingly difficult for the couple to satisfy each other's changing and maturing motivations.

In addition to the changing life styles, new experiences, new learning, and new acquaintances can conspire to change us in broad and unpredictable ways. The radical can become reactionary. The parentally-influenced Republican can become a peer-influenced anarchist. The shy introvert may suddenly discover the joys of an outgoing life, or the extrovert find the satisfaction of quietude. Unless both lovers make these changes together, they will find themselves sharing less and less of their lives. In short, as a couple's needs change, they can find themselves needing each other less.

We do not know exactly how often people move away from each other in this way, nor how much this contributes to divorce and separation. We see it happening frequently, and it is most certainly important. It is, of course, not inevitable. Although people change with age, they can age together. It seems more likely that a couple will change in the same direction than grow completely apart. If they change together, then it is probable that they will at least make some effort to continue to reinforce each other. Love is an investment. Time and effort are sown, and warmth, companionship, and affection are reaped. The investment is worth protecting, but a deliberate and determined effort is often necessary. Good marriages are characterized by changing together (particularly by the wife's changing to resemble her husband more closely, see Chapter IX); bad marriages, by changing apart.

*Changing Attractiveness: The Myths of Aging*

Most couples meet and fall in love when they are quite young. Often, of course, physical beauty forms an important part of the initial attractiveness. Youth (particularly feminine) is beautiful and sexually attractive; old age is, at best, dignified. Television and movies constantly remind us that Lotharios pursue barely postpubescent belles for their bodies and matrons for their money. A middle-aged Miss Universe is unheard of. Youth is ravishing and age ravishes.

Although both men and women grow older, it is clearly the woman who is viewed as being the more vulnerable to the effects of aging. The 45-year-old man is often perceived as youthful, suave, sophisticated, and perhaps, distinguished. The 45-year-old woman is usually described as middle aged. As our attractiveness is weakened by age, so is some of our reinforcement value to our mates. It is not uncommon to find men marrying successively younger women in an apparent attempt to exhibit to all a sexually attractive and coveted partner.

It is an ironic, partly economic, accident that maturity is frequently a man's attribute but a woman's handicap; for in purely biological terms, nothing could be further from the truth. Women not only live longer than men (about seven years longer on the average) but they also reach their sexual peaks much later (at an age when men are on the downhill slope). The female hormones (estrogens) that are produced by the premenopausal woman afford her insulation from the physically debilitating effects of age by partially protecting her heart and blood vessels from sclerotic disease. Therefore, in a very real sense, women can be said to age more slowly than men. Why then, do we so clearly respond as though the opposite were true? We can only speculate.

It has been traditional in our culture, as well as in most others, that the male carries the responsibility for the economic security of the family. This makes it necessary for the man to achieve a certain station in life before becoming eligible to marry. As education and training require more and more time in a society, the difference between male marital readiness and female eligibility (which usually takes no more time than physical maturity) becomes exaggerated.

Thus, we come to associate older men with younger women. In addition, men reach economic, political, or professional prominence and, therefore, the public eye, far more often than do women. There are many more male scientists, business figures, and politicians than female. Usually, the sort of prominence that leads to public exposure in the mass media is not achieved until middle age, and therefore, public figures (usually men) who are in their forties are perceived as young. In fact, they are, relative to their prominence. As so often decried by women's liberation movements, women who do achieve celebrity status, often do so as sex objects and are displayed only in order to expose face and figure. This requires no lengthy training to achieve.

So we add to the subtle concepts we learn about age. The forties are old for women (psychologically, not biologically) and young (psychologically, not biologically) for men. Sometimes the simple biological mismatch that results when the 30-year-old wife is limited to her 40-year-old husband's sexual interest contributes to unhappiness, infidelity, and divorce.

## The Aftermath

For whatever reason or combination of reasons, love often turns to indifference or even antipathy. The company of our mates is simply no longer reinforcing. And, quite frequently, we look to pastures that seem greener. The promise of freedom beckons; its associated problems relatively mute from the distance. With divorce, and the formation of a new union, we discover all too often that this new pasture, too, has weeds.

Most divorces are not legally contested, implying at least some agreement. In California, the law now reads exactly that way—mutual consent is sufficient grounds. It seems likely that this pattern will take on nationwide adoption in the not-too-distant future.

Having dissolved one marriage, the divorced person seems incredibly eager to regain the state just vacated. At all ages, the divorced person is far more likely to marry (again) than one who has never been married. And this trend increases with age. Eighty-nine percent of never-married women at 20 will marry eventually; 93% of 20-year-old divorcees will remarry. At 30, the figures become 48% for the single person and 94% for the divorcee. At 40, they are 16% and 65% respectively; and at 45, 9% and 50% (Landis, 1970, pp. 651–652).

The same holds true for men, who are slightly more likely to marry than women whether single, divorced, or widowed. Widows (and widowers) are also more likely to marry than single people, but not as likely as divorcees. These facts can be interpreted in several ways. Undoubtedly, there is a selection factor operating. People who marry once show some willingness to do so and also an ability to attract a partner. Their negative experience with one marriage doesn't seem to make them gun-shy for a second try. The fact that age for age, divorced people are more likely to remarry (and remarry far sooner) than the widowed, probably reflects the fact that some marriages are broken by affairs which in turn culminate in marriage. It also seems reasonable to assume that the loss of a mate through death is far more traumatic and punishing than the shedding of an unwanted mate by divorce. Perhaps both contribute to the effect. In any case, the data suggest that, to men and women, marriage teaches a need for marriage; for, overwhelmingly, people rapidly regain that state if it is lost. Once married, we undoubtedly learn the benefits of the help and company of another person. If we lose this close relationship, we experience loneliness and we seek someone to fill the void. Once again, the tendency to act (in this case, remarry) arises out of the fact that distance diminishes painful problems more than pleasures.

Evidently, for some people, shuttling in and out of marriage becomes a behavior pattern. The more divorces a married couple has in their history, the more likely it is that they themselves will divorce (Landis, 1970). Perhaps some people are simply divorce-prone because they cannot form deep and mutually rewarding attachments. It is also likely that each succeeding divorce is simply easier than the last. It is not so much that people fail to learn through the experience of a bad marriage, but that they adapt to the terrors of separating. It seems to us, that whatever excitement and pleasure there may be in this serial succession of partners; it is more than counteracted for most people by the loss of the benefits of a close, long-standing, and growing love relationship. Certainly, people who divorce several times are spending a significant proportion of their lives in avoidance and escape behavior.

## Monotony: Love Killer

Many years ago, one of us (Siegel and Pilgrim, 1958) conducted an experiment designed to examine the influence of repetition on the acceptability of food. Three times a day, in a small mess hall, college students were served nutritionally well-balanced meals, rated entirely palatable at the outset. Two daily menus were alternated, so that every other day, the exact same menu came up again. Throughout the experiment, each subject was asked to rate the palatability (tastiness) of each food item. Within six days (three servings), the ratings began to decline. By the end of 22 days (11 servings), the decline in rated palatability had become quite marked. Throughout the experiment, progressively more food was left uneaten, and more and more subjects dropped from the study. Needless to add, the cost of eating is no small part of the college student's budget. This experiment clearly demonstrated that even as basic an action as eating possesses the capability of generating its own inhibition.

Many psychological theorists fully believe that it is very much a part of the human condition that repetition of any and every activity must ultimately bring on a sense of monotony or boredom and the impulse to turn away or escape. No matter how rewarding the initial experience and despite continued reinforcement, if repeated often enough, the activity will ultimately pale or grow stale. Whether it be eating steaks, luxuriating in the sun and fun of the most elegant resort, listening to the most exciting symphony, or dallying with a delightful mermaid, repetition will finally turn us away.

Must love go this route? Is it inevitable that the love relationship must ultimately collapse beneath the burden of monotony? Many people seem to believe this. We do not. At the same time, we acknowledge that the monotony principle is a sound one. There is no contradiction here. Monotony comes about with invariant experience. Throughout this book, we have stressed the central role played by unpredictable reinforcement. We have insisted that approach behaviors (and love) are sustained and strengthened by rewarding experiences that vary in kind and in frequency; that is, reinforcing experiences that are not completely predictable. And, in Chapter IX, a great deal of attention was given to the necessity of breaking routine in the preservation of a happy marriage.

In the present chapter, so far, loss of love has been pretty much tied to changing needs that render our lovers ineffective as reinforcers. We must now make explicit another cause of loss of love, one that has been implicit all along. It is monotony coming in the door that drives love out the window. In the absence of any dramatic change in our personal and social needs, love will still falter if the interaction between two lovers becomes stereotyped and invariant. Variety is indeed the spice of life. Our capacity to maintain the love relationship is limited, then, by the personal (and economic) resources we can bring to bear on the production of day-to-day variation in the interaction with our lovers. We close the chapter on that point.

SUGGESTED READING

Krich, A., & Blum, S. Marriage and the mystique of romance. *Redbook Magazine*, November, 1970, pp. 65, 118, 120–121, 123.

Landis, P. H. *Making the most of marriage*. (4th edition) New York: Appleton-Century-Crofts, 1970. Especially the chapters on divorce and remarriage.

CHAPTER XI

# Other Loves

SUMMARY

There are many loves aside from the erotic love of man for woman. We love children, friends, and pets. In other ways, it could be said that we love some things that are not even living beings, such as the home in which we live, or the abstraction we call mankind. The differences lie in the types of reinforcement involved and the degree of generalization of the love response.

Parents begin to love children largely because our society expects them to. To do otherwise would be to court severe social sanction. Once we experience parenthood, the very difficulty of child rearing can make us feel that we really want the tribulations that circumstances force us to accept. Then, too, children, provide substantial rewards. They validate our worth, at first by merely needing us, and eventually by adopting our characteristics, our teachings, and our beliefs.

Pets are almost substitute children, and can be loved dearly. While not as capable as a human being of giving us complicated and varied reinforcement, they accept us completely and uncritically and thus engender in us intense feelings of attraction.

Friendship is an important chapter in human development, particularly during adolescence. Friends share many explorations and pleasures with each other and teach us the ways of getting along with other people, and of securing social approval.

Love of humanity is partly a generalization from many experiences with different people and partly the fulfillment of the equivocal social expectation that we should at least talk as though we loved all people. Inanimate objects can be loved only in a much narrower way than love for people. Homes are varied and complex enough to develop in us a kind of love response, but perhaps no other nonliving objects are.

119

Abstract principles can be admired and followed and they may become very important to us, but we do not love abstractions in the sense we have been using.

This book is mostly about the romantic love of man for woman, and woman for man. But there are other kinds and forms of love, some commonplace and "natural," others labeled neurotic or abnormal. There can be love objects other than the opposite sex. We can direct and express our love in many ways. In earlier chapters, we alluded to brotherly love, fatherly love, love of God, love of pets, etc. And we have given a great deal of attention to motherly love. We suggested quite early that the principles offered as an account of love are general in operation, and that the differences among various types of love are to be found in the differing kinds of reinforcing experiences.

Love within a family group can be accounted for by applying the principles of learning. Families in our society are constituted as units of mutual enhancement. Add to this the fact that values are more nearly similar within families than between them (through both hereditary and environmental factors), and you have the basis for a strongly learned "familial" love. Some of the relationships within a family have special meaning in addition to this, however. The love of parents for children, for example, is deserving of special consideration. In any case, though the general principles of love are similar, the specific circumstances of the relationship define the type of love. We turn in the next three chapters to a fuller development of this point; to a longer look at some of the other kinds of love; from those found in everyday family relationships to the half-hidden sexual loves of man for man and woman for woman.

As we examine other love relationships, we shall try to describe the pattern of reinforcement associated with each type of love object. It is the kind of reward we obtain from each different love object that gives it a unique identity. We want to know just what needs are met in interaction with the love object that give each relationship its particular flavor.

### Parental Love

We have said a great deal about motherly love, and a bit about fatherly love (especially in Chapters IV and V). In both instances, however, the mother or the father was object, not subject. We were really talking about love *for* the mother and love *for* the father—the parents as objects of the child's love. The importance of this love was stressed as it contributed to the development of later love relationships. The all-expecting and demanding love of children for their parents, wherein the child has not yet fully learned the satisfactions of giving, is appropriate in this early relationship. It is when we do not progress from this type of love to a more nearly give and take relationship as adults that we display what has been termed neurotic love. That is, the demanding love of a child becomes neurotic love if continued as an adult.

But the parent-child relationship is a two-way street and it is now time to reverse the question. What about the parents as the subjects of loving, and the child as the object? Since we have discussed love for parents as a relatively selfish kind of love, our task now becomes that of describing the ways in which the child rewards the parents. What does the child give that encourages the approach behavior of the parents that we call love for children?

Most animals tend their offspring expertly from the moment of delivery, whether it be the first litter or the fifth. Learning or practice is unnecessary. Some would generalize from lower animals to man and suggest that the behavior of the human mother in tending her infant is also instinctively given. We doubt this. Hit and miss is too often the case, and the mother's cry, "What do I do now?" is the rule, not the exception. Clinics on infant care usually play to a full house. Apparently, mothers (and fathers) must learn through experience. Parenthood doesn't just come naturally.

Before we examine the development of parental love for children, there is a prior question to answer. Why do people have children in the first place? We are speaking of the planned or wanted baby, of course. The accidental by-product of a sexual union scarcely requires explanation.

We want children for many and varied reasons. We are aware of some of these reasons; some go unspoken or unrecognized. Usually, more than one motive operates. Our children can represent many things to us: a hold on immortality (continuation of the self or, much the same thing, continuation of the family name), an economic investment (potential future breadwinner), a retirement plan (old age's caretaker), a needed love object to fill the vacuum in an otherwise loveless marriage. And, there are others. Perhaps the strongest single reason is found in the social requirements. We are expected to grow up, marry, and have children. It's as simple as that. We fulfill, usually unthinkingly, the role society demands of us; a role most of us have learned to accept.

Once the baby arrives, it's a different ball game. The responsibility of constant care and attention becomes the chronic burden of the mother. The father must now share his wife's affection and time, and make sacrifices in his style of living or in his personal economy. Babies are demanding; children only slightly less so. Aside from the occasional burst of reinforcement that attends the prideful exhibition of the new baby, infant care is, at best, trying; at worst, quite aversive. But, gradually, the costs give way to the gains. Out of the tending relationship, dictated by a sense of responsibility more than anything else, there grows genuine affection. Most of us come to cherish and hold dear that which we have cared for, nurtured, and made sacrifices for, whether it be a goldfish, a puppy, or a child. Often, the greater the sacrifices, the stronger the attachment. The love of parents, especially the mother, for a mentally or physically handicapped child is a not uncommon, and always heart-rending, scene. It is as though the more demanding the caring responsibility, the stronger the affection. Sensitivity to the helplessness of the child is also very much a part of this relationship.

In some measure, the affection of parent for child stems from the operation of a principle known as cognitive dissonance (Festinger, 1957), which we discussed informally in Chapter III when describing poor self-concepts. We usually hold dear any unpleasantness that circumstances compel us to accept. We are quite likely to interpret favorably the exasperating demands necessarily made upon us by our children. In this interpretation, we give the child's behavior a humorous twist or discover in it some value. And our sacrifices become "all for the good." In other words, our attitudes toward the child change in such a fashion as to make more meaningful the many unwanted responsibilities thrust upon us. In this way, the "dissonance," or the contradictions in our behavior (ready acceptance of unpleasant responsibilities), are reduced.

Children serve as another potent source of reinforcement. So to speak, they validate us. They feed back our cherished attitudes, feelings, and beliefs. There are exceptions, of course, but quite generally, Catholics rear Catholic children, and Protestants, Protestants; Republicans, Republicans, and Democrats, Democrats. The conservative economic policy of the father is likely to be seen in his son and his daughter. Or the liberal social philosophy of the mother is reflected in the attitudes of her children. This is all true at least throughout the early years. With maturity and developing independence, the attitudes, feelings, and beliefs of the younger generation may diverge, of course. Sometimes (it is still the exception, not the rule), the turnabout is complete—180 degrees. This becomes the source of quietly suffered disappointment and chagrin in some parents; disaffection and alienation in others.

Most parents identify in some degree with their children. At times, all of us feel pride in the achievements of our children. We brag about their successes and we rationalize their failures. We act just a little bit as if the accomplishments of the child are really our own accomplishments; his failures, our failures. Up to a limit, this may be considered quite normal. Beyond a point, however, this relationship becomes an unhealthy one, destructive of both parents and child. Parents often entertain ambitions for the child that completely ignore his needs and wishes. His inclinations to the contrary, the child is pointed in the direction of this or that occupation or profession. The parent thus compensates for his own sense of inadequacy, almost always without realizing his true motivation. The parent asks (or demands) that the child accomplish a station in life that fulfills the parent, not the child. In the realm of sports, this is a common scene. The father who didn't quite make it on the baseball diamond, the tennis court, or the gridiron, pushes his boy hard in that direction at the first show of even mild interest. On a broad scale, Little League baseball is the example, *par excellence*, of this kind of parental compensation. Five minutes attendance at one of these overheated spectacles should persuade the most casual observer that the game is designed to fulfill parents, not children. The child is merely the agent of parental expression.

In the extreme, yet not infrequent instance, a parent may totally merge his identity with that of the child. The parent gives up his own thing, surrenders his own development and uniqueness, and "lives only for the children." This spectacle is sadder than Little League baseball, for this parent is training himself for later total dependence on the child—a relationship far more likely to generate resentment, than affection.

### Love of Pets

Sometimes the recommendation is made by a psychiatrist or psychologist that, before having a baby, the newly married couple first adopt and raise a puppy. This becomes the testing arena for parenthood. The young couple will come to know firsthand the problems and sacrifices, the satisfactions and the joys, of caring for a helpless living creature. This advice makes good sense. There is little question that this experience may well gauge both the adequacy and the readiness for parenthood. And the practice should be quite valuable.

It cannot be disputed that many of us love an animal in the true sense of the verb. We care for, cherish, feel tenderness toward, and often make sacrifices for pets. We miss them when absent. And we grieve deeply at their deaths. There exists no more moving account of bereavement than Loudon Wainwright's "Another Sort of Love Story" (*Life*, January 22, 1971) in which he tells of his feelings and his recollections upon the death of his dog, John Henry.

In some people, the affection for a pet has such extreme expression as to form the basis for broad social ridicule or, at best, wry humor. We refer with a giggle to the old maid and her cats. The probated will that turns up a cat or a dog as sole heir to a substantial fortune is scarcely newsworthy any longer. The couple, always or recently childless, whose solicitude for an animal equals that expressed by few parents for their children, is no rarity. There are canine millinery shops, maternity wards, and cemeteries. The commercial preparation of varied menus designed to titillate the pet's palate is a thriving business. Psychiatric treatment is available to dogs in some of our larger cities. You can buy a fancy dog casket in all but the smallest towns. This all adds up to either idiocy or love. Maybe both.

How do we account for this love direction? In what ways do pets reinforce us? What human needs are fulfilled in this relationship? The answer lies largely in the old saying that "A dog is a man's best friend." It's no accident that it's the dog that's featured in this proverb. More than any other pet, it is the dog that most strongly expresses loyalty and devotion, that returns what we most want—love. He is there. He is uncomplaining and uncritical; neither carper nor critic. There's never doubt about where you stand with him. We claim his time at will. And for this he is grateful; he soaks up affection. Almost in caricature, this relationship reflects man's need to love, to be loved, and to be accepted uncritically. There lies the reinforcing power of pets.

Certainly the variety of reward (and its unpredictability) is less from pets than from humans. And, as a consequence, our love for them, though at times intense, is not as broad as our love for people.

Mourning in their absence or loss is powerful but not as pervasive as mourning for a lost loved person. Nevertheless, the enormity and strength of our need to be uncritically accepted and loved directs a powerful attraction toward pets. Much of the value they lose because of their relatively uncomplicated natures, they regain because this very simplicity demands so little and delivers so much.

## Friendship

Attachment to, and respect and affection for a particular member of the same sex we call friendship; it is most certainly a form of love. Although most of us enjoy, in some degree, friendships (with both sexes) in adulthood, it is in preadolescence and adolescence that this relationship has its most intense expression. At some time during the grammar school years, most children begin to seek the almost exclusive companionship of one other particular child of like sex. And they become chums. They form a two-group that is a kind of closed society; third parties are either treated as intruders or ignored.

Chums enjoy an intimate and deep social union, a relationship that qualifies as one of life's most meaningful, most valuable, and most satisfying experiences. They share common pursuits and common goals. There is a give and take to their activities; each adjusts his behavior to the other. They suffer failures together, they relish the same accomplishments, and they borrow each other's prestige. This is love in a very meaningful sense—chums exhibit, for the first time in life, a genuine sensitivity to the needs and concerns of another human being. This, of course, stands in sharp contrast to the earlier one-way, no give, all-demanding social orientation of the preschool child.

The lesson learned in these early pervasive and intense friendships are profound ones. In brief, chums teach each other just what it takes to get along smoothly with members of the same sex. Those unfortunate persons who, for one reason or another, never form this close relationship during childhood, probably never will. And these are the people most likely to experience awkwardness in their adult lives in social exchange with members of the same sex (and, for that matter, with the opposite sex).

A unique characteristic of the chum relationship is what might be called mutual mirroring. Out of the intimacy of the relationship, there usually develops, for the first time, some capacity on the part of the child to see himself as others see him. And his self-image changes as a result. Through the eyes of his close friend, he perceives the significance of his own actions; he senses his social errors and he experiences more strongly the impact of social reality. His deep need for acceptance (the primary motivation that accounts for chumming) requires that he make amends when his behavior strains the relationship; to do otherwise is to risk the loss of this treasured acceptance. In learning how to get along with the one, the child usually learns how to get along with the many of later living. In the thinking of the renowned psychiatrist, Harry Stack Sullivan (1953), mutual mirroring and the consequent social reorientation that results from it may go a long way toward correcting unhealthy social habits learned in an overindulgent, overprotective, or harsh early home environment.

The intense quality of the chum relationship is sometimes the occasion for unjustified alarm on the part of parents. They feel that it "goes too far." In some instances, parental concern is rooted in simple jealousy. The parent is basically unwilling to share the child's time and affection, and is just a bit resentful when he expresses preference for the company of another child. In other instances, the parent is responding to a fear of deviantly developing sexuality. Especially true of boys, the chum relationship typically includes sexual exploration. For example, mutual masturbation is probably the rule, not the exception. Discovery of such activities is likely to alarm the parents on two counts: overconcern with masturbation (always, of course, the leader is the "outside" child) and fear of like-sexed intimacy as homosexual in character. Case histories of male homosexuals, however, usually reveal a childhood singularly devoid of chum relationships. The homosexual is more likely one who failed to form such an early intimate friendship with another male of the same age. In the opinion of Harry Stack Sullivan (1953), adult homosexuality and the intimacy of chumming are negatively, not positively, related.

What are the sources of reinforcement in this form of love that we call friendship? What rewarding experiences draw together two members of the same sex whether chums of childhood or friends of adulthood? The answer is much the same in both stages of life. However, the reasons are more easily discerned in the case of the child, who is more likely to be open and honest, or less guarded, than the adult. We shall analyze the child. We can generalize to the adult.

When the child enters school, he breaks for the first time from the protective environment of the home. He leaves behind a solicitous mother and confronts a discipline imposed by a teacher who makes demands and insists on their acceptance; and whose attention is shared with many others. He must abandon his cherished narrow and selfish pursuits and accommodate to the needs and purposes of the group. If he does not sometimes give (or better still, give in), he risks ostracism —isolation, alienation, and consequent loneliness. This is without doubt a severely challenging, even traumatic, experience for the child. It is a chapter of life fraught with uncertainty, pain, and threat. And the child more or less naturally seeks out another human being to form a buffer, a social union that serves to lessen the impact of these experiences. This is a primary motivation involved in the development of the relationship we call friendship. And the general principle holds in adulthood as well. Friends ease the trials and tribulations of life.

A close friend also serves to validate personal worth. That we can hold, influence, and be deeply appreciated by another human being clearly demonstrates that we are worthwhile.

There is another reason for chumming. The grammar school years are years of extremely active exploration of the world. To the child this world is unknown, even mysterious, but it is also beckoning. The risks and uncertainties attending this exploration are far less formidable when shared.

Many authorities view friendship as a direct reflection of man's deep need for personal intimacy—as though instinctively dictated. Perhaps this is so, but the evidence is hard to come by. The experience of helplessness in infancy and early childhood would seem to go a long way toward establishing a learned basis for this need (Chapter V).

## Love's Higher Moments

We have talked about love between people, and briefly of love for pets, but we have not yet directly addressed the issue of the broad use of the word, "love." We hear of love for Humanity, God, and Justice. We speak loosely of love for inanimate objects such as houses, cars, and even types of food. Can we truly love such things? And if so, in what sense? To answer these questions, we must reexamine our definition of love rather closely.

Love is a strong generalized approach response to a stimulus that has been diversely and somewhat unpredictably associated with reward. The stimulus becomes a signal for imminent pleasure; hope is aroused. We have taken for granted the reader's intuitive grasp of the nature of a stimulus. We have implied that a stimulus is necessarily some physical object or event and, in the instance of a love stimulus, that it must be quite a complex one, such as a living person, or, at least, an intelligent living pet. But food is not a complex stimulus, nor is it animate. An abstract principle is not even a physical object. Can we love things? There are two separate questions involved here—complexity and concreteness. We shall address the easier of the two first.

Inanimate objects are rarely complicated enough to be diversely and unpredictably rewarding. Regardless of what we do with them, we can usually predict the outcome, and hence, we use them only under restricted circumstances. Moreover, granted sanity, we do not believe that inanimate objects love, accept, and desire us. This strips objects of a most important source of reinforcement. At most, we can need inanimate objects, we can use them, we can enjoy them, and we may even admire them; but, in general, we cannot truly love them. Perhaps a possible exception to this, is a home. Because of the many and varied activities that we enjoy in our homes, we can come to feel pleasure in simply occupying that particular house. We often end up preferring that particular house to others that could serve our basic needs just as well. And this preference, this general approach, along with the feelings of pleasure and comfort we experience when there, qualifies as a type of love. It is, at least, a borderline case.

In spite of our rather broad application of the word "love," however, other inanimate objects do not inspire such a feeling. We can like food, cars, jewelry, and machines; but in no meaningful sense do we love them.

What of qualities, ideas or, as psychologists often call them, abstractions? Can we love these?

This is a complicated question, for it raises a central issue in psychological theory: "What is the nature of an abstraction?" We are really talking here about something we mentioned earlier. As human beings, we are capable of responding to types of stimuli that vary in complexity from that afforded by a single concrete object to that inherent in a highly abstract principle. On the basis of certain similarities, we group into categories objects that may be widely different in other ways. We called this concept formation (Chapter II). A single, particular, round, red ball forms a highly specific and narrow category. Similarly, all round, red balls may become a category, as may all balls, and finally, even all round objects. In moving from one particular ball to all round objects, we are generalizing more and more broadly. We learn to respond to such general concepts as roundness, but the response weakens as the stimuli become less and less similar to the original concretely experienced object. So we may learn to love a single human being and, with enough reinforcing experiences with enough human beings, we may generalize our love to all people or most people. But the discriminated love of one human for another is a response that is really of a different order from this kind of generalized love of all the humans we meet.

Love for Humanity in the abstract, however, is not quite so simply explained. There is much more to the phenomenon. We are taught (with some inconsistency) quite directly to say and to convince ourselves that we are warm, people-loving creatures. Religions, philosophies, and systems of ethics teach us to love Humanity—or, at least, to say that we do. We are rewarded by the approval of our parents, teachers, and friends for expressions of such an all-encompassing love. It becomes a part of our ideal selves. Unfortunately, actions expressive of this love (generosity, forgiveness, and acceptance, for example) are as often punished by circumstances and by other people as they are rewarded. And we develop a split between what we say about love for mankind, and how we actually act toward people in general.

There are, then, somewhat separable aspects to love for Humanity. We can quite directly learn a need for and an approach to people in general as a consequence of generalizing from early rewarding experiences. Additionally, we may learn intellectually the desirability of exhibiting a superficial verbal expression of love for all mankind. But the actions that speak louder than words rarely follow.

### Love of Country

What of other kinds of abstractions? Is an ideal the same as the love for a principle? Is patriotism love for country? We can apply the same analysis to these questions that we have just applied to home and Humanity.

Let us illustrate with love of country. Surely, a part of the feeling we have for the country in which we live is generalized from the feeling about our homes. This represents quite a broad generalization. However, it is difficult to form an intense response to so vast a stimulus, and so, to account for strongly felt patriotism, we must look elsewhere. Of course, part of the explanation lies in the kind of social expectancy that we have just described in love for Humanity, but there is more. We react to some things (such as our country) as though they were parts of ourselves. Glory to our country reflects glory on us; the success of the nation is our success. Psychologists call this identification, and it is an important determinant of our responses to many different things; particularly, countries, home towns, football teams and, as we saw earlier, our children.

## Abstractions

Love for Truth, Beauty, God, and other abstractions cannot be said to be love in the meaning used throughout this book. For the most part, these are ideals that we may strongly admire and wish to make a part of ourselves, or even seek as experiences, but they are too abstract to love as we define the word. Obviously, there are many such abstractions and they mean different things to different people. Some of these can become very important to us and can shape our lives. We can base a great deal of our living on the effort to follow such abstract principles. And we can approve of, and perhaps even love, ourselves and others more inasmuch as we can successfully live up to certain of these ideals. In this sense, but only in this sense, can we be said to love such highly abstract concepts. The personification of such abstractions (as in many religious interpretations of God) can be loved only in the way that we intensely yearn for a never really directly experienced fantasy or image. Although this generates feeling and may direct much of our behavior, it is still not love as we have defined it.

SUGGESTED READING

Sullivan, H. S. *The interpersonal theory of psychiatry*. H. S. Perry and M. L. Gawell (Eds.), New York: Norton, 1953, Chapter 16.

# CHAPTER XII

# Love Awry

## SUMMARY

The concept of abnormality in love is an elusive one. It is best for our purposes to define abnormal behavior in terms of impaired efficiency of our actions in satisfying our needs. Abnormality is partly a function of the culture that defines it.

In the area of love, we see a variety of behaviors that are, in some sense, abnormal. The total inability to love is perhaps the most basic and it can arise from several causes, most important of which are: lack of the early learning experience necessary to develop the bases of love, fear of intimacy, or an unusually critical self-perception. Repeated patterns of apparent love-seeking (such as "Don Juanism," or compulsive female promiscuity) also signal difficulties in forming satisfying love relationships. Again, low self-esteem is a frequent cause of these problems.

Although some amount of jealousy is normal in our culture, it has several extreme forms. Insecurity and projection are often important mechanisms behind pathologically jealous reactions.

Love relationship problems usually manifest themselves in sexual expression. Normal sexual functioning can be interfered with in many ways. Adequate sexual stimulation can be blocked by either the male or female as a result of anxiety, fear, hostility, or other factors both personal and interpersonal. Fear of inadequacy is undoubtedly the greatest single cause of sexual dysfunction, followed by guilt, interpersonal hostility, and rejection. When either partner suffers from sexual dysfunction, the relationship is always adversely affected. Successful treatment necessitates working with the relationship between the couple, rather than the individuals singly.

Love exists in many degrees, takes many objects and many forms. In so-called normal development, we love a wide variety of people in manifold ways. All of these experiences are neither equally rewarding nor equally desirable. Our society does not view all types of love with the same degree of acceptance. George may be encouraged to love his mother, allowed to love Mary, but forbidden to express an erotic love for Fred. We, ostensibly at least, define this last love as "abnormal." Our culture tells us that heterosexual adultery is "normal," but homosexual attachments, even among consenting adults, are "abnormal." Nor is choice of object the only way in which love can be classified as abnormal. Expression becomes another criterion. Sexual abstinence between lovers is usually described as normal, but impotence or frigidity as abnormal. Many love behaviors are considered normal in one set of circumstances and abnormal in another. Time, place, and frequency are determinants of the cultural acceptance of many things. Before we attempt an analysis of what might be called the pathology of love, we must address the question of what we mean by "abnormal."

If we proceed under the assumption that all behavior is lawful in the sense that it follows predictably from certain antecedent events (and we do, indeed, assume this), then abnormal clearly cannot mean uncaused or "unnatural." Loving is interpersonal behavior, and thus highly dependent on social rewards and punishments. If loving is learned, then abnormal loving must also be learned. The same principles apply whether the behavior is socially approved or condemned, adaptive, or destructive. The difference lies in different circumstances. Adaptive, socially approved acts, are more likely to meet with reward than socially disapproved behavior; and thus, the latter must be dependent on some subculture or uncommon social milieu for a source of interpersonal reinforcement.

To some extent then, our definition of abnormal is cultural and relative, based on degree of acceptance within a given social group. Although cultural acceptance is a necessary part of our definition, it is neither complete nor completely accurate. For one thing, it begs the question of why some behavior is approved by a given group and some condemned. For another, it raises the issue of whether or not a culture itself can in some sense be "abnormal." These are big questions. And since we are not interested as much here in the concept of abnormality *per se* as we are in what can go wrong with love, we shall only suggest broad working definitions that will describe the framework needed for our purposes.

Simply put, learning is the mechanism that modifies behavior to more effectively satisfy needs in a changing environment. And yet, many times we behave in ways that are destructive to ourselves and to others. Sometimes, we repeatedly act maladaptively even when, apparently, we have more desirable options open to us. Behavior that does disservice to our needs is, to the extent of that disservice, abnormal. Since we are not ideal organisms, none of our behavior is likely to be perfect. Therefore, we must add a statistical qualification to our definition of abnormality. It is only the extremes of maladaptive behavior that fit this category.

This broad definition allows us to address the issues raised above. Can cultures themselves be abnormal in some ways? Yes, it is certainly possible for a culture to teach us behaviors that actually interfere with need satisfaction. Parts of India are chronically faced with food shortages and yet cows are viewed there as sacred animals, not to be eaten. This culture is teaching behavior of disservice to need. There is a built-in conflict; choice between semistarvation and social punishment. Here is another example, more strongly related to our argument: Western society teaches us conflicting social needs. Adolescent boys are taught to be daring, aggressive, sexually successful Lotharios on the one hand, and considerate, chaste, gentlemanly, and highly moral on the other. It is most difficult to satisfy both roles simultaneously and, therefore, conflict and frustration are built in; hence "abnormality."

To a major extent, then, social approval and disapproval do, in fact, define abnormality. That is, society forces upon us certain ways of behaving that do not efficiently serve our needs. For the most part, of course, society approves those actions that are compatible with the best interests of the group, and condemns those that are destructive of these interests. But not always. Many customs and values are hangovers from the past. Perhaps they were once functional; perhaps some are off-shoots of the political system. In any case, much of our behavior is governed by rules of conduct that fail to serve any obvious constructive purpose. The realms of love and sex seem especially vulnerable to this kind of control. Our love behaviors are enmeshed in a network of often arbitrary regulations and demands. For this reason there are many possible pitfalls—ways in which love can go awry.

We are not interested in cataloguing sexual disorders. Rather, we are concerned with deviant interpersonal relationships. And yet it is in the sexual realm, within this one type of love expression, that society maintains the greatest influence. Two men may love, but they must not sexually desire each other. Familial love is approved, but within the family, sex is condemned. Thus, any discussion of wayward love necessarily focuses heavily on sex. We shall choose our topics for discussion with a principal focus on the psychology of the love relationship. Sexual deviation will necessarily overlap somewhat with this and, therefore, cannot be ignored.

## The Inability to Love

Undoubtedly, the most basic disorder of love is its chronic total absence. Some people cannot love. All conscious human beings can learn and can respond to conditioned reinforcers. Such being the case, it follows that all people should, if given the opportunity, become capable of loving. That this is not true implies the operation of some mechanism capable of inhibiting normal development of the ability to love. More likely, there are several such mechanisms, some of them dealing directly with past experience in love situations, and perhaps some a bit more indirectly. Let's begin with the former.

Chapter V traced some of the important early social interactions of the infant. The way in which a helpless baby first experiences need gratification was stressed as critical in learning dependence upon, and eventually love for, another human being. If the mother is firmly established as a signal for relief, gratification, and pleasure, then the foundation is established for moving toward other people. Human beings in general come to signal pleasurable expectancies. The first year of life is particularly important in this learning. Typically, there are few demands made on the infant during the first year. His discomforts are internal and relieved, not brought about, by other people. The second year, however, introduces aversive social control. Society begins to demand conformity, and the same agents (people—especially the mother) who formerly signaled relief or pleasure now dish out punishment as well. If the first year did not afford sufficient opportunity for learning a hopeful dependency, no generalizations can take place, and people are not sought later as reinforcing objects. Since they did not become conditioned hope signals during this very critical early stage of learning, their presence does not prove rewarding. Less time will be spent in social interaction, and this unhappy adult will very likely develop a pathological (in our society) self-sufficiency—thus shutting off opportunity to gain, in later life, the lost positive learning experience.

Even if the first year goes well with respect to the development of dependency and pleasurable expectation, the punishment of the second year can be a harsh and cruel teacher of disappointment. The mother (or father) who fails to temper the necessary demands of socialization by continuing as a predominantly positively reinforcing stimulus, who is overly punitive, can teach the infant that his early trust was misplaced. The child now learns that it is dangerous to place too much faith in the "good nature" of people. This unfortunate child has first learned to need people, only to discover later that he cannot trust them. What agony this can bring when he experiences, as an adult, a return of this fear whenever he gets too close to someone. Most of us know at least someone who runs from or destroys any relationship that becomes (for him) threateningly intimate.

To a lesser extent, when appropriate learning of early love relationships has taken place, any negative experience with loved ones will tend to introduce some fear, and therefore, some inhibition of approach toward potential love objects. In the adult who has developed his early love relationship fully, however, recovery from disappointment and rejection is rapid and complete. "Hope springs eternal" in a very real sense.

A somewhat different difficulty that may interfere with an adult's ability to love arises out of the self-perception that we discussed briefly in Chapters III and VI. We described how low self-esteem can interfere with the ability to accept love. An inability to accept love is a serious handicap in loving, or in giving love. An individual suffering from low self-esteem is likely to devalue anyone who thinks highly of him. It is easy to see that this devaluation would make it difficult to love that person. A major part of his reward value is lost. He is no longer viewed as valuable or desirable and so his attention cannot be truly gratifying. The net result in the extreme case of this learned disorder is that unrequited love is the only kind open to the victim; for once his love is returned, the value of the giver is lowered.

The fabled unrequited love, sung by bards and storied by poets, is a lonely affair. A true love relationship involves reciprocal reinforcement-giving and getting. Pleasure is derived from both. How rewarding it is to be able to please someone in many ways and, at the same time, to have that person wish to please you. Unrequited love is, at best, merely a yearning for a potential relationship; at worst, a neurotic need that, by its very nature, cannot be fulfilled. Unrequited love, of course, is no love at all.

## Don Juanism

A disorder not unrelated to the complete inability to love is the neurotic need to make sexual conquest. In the light of earlier discussions in this book, the reader might justifiably ask, at this point, why varied sexual experience is being considered abnormal. It is not, as such. We are not referring to the truly "liberated" person, either male or female, who can and does form true love relationships but who also enjoys a variety of nonexploitative sexual affairs. This can be an enviable and happy individual. Unfortunately, he is also a rare individual in our culture. Our society's built-in conflicts over sex, double standards, hypocrisy, and simple condemnation, make it most difficult for sexual libertarianism to be without emotional cost.

There are no reliable data available on exactly how many "happily liberated" people there are. But the data we do have suggest that the number is small. We wish this were not true. But it is, and as a consequence we find that sexual liberalism, instead of promoting happiness and adjustment as one might predict from the fact that it is the satisfaction of an important need, is often associated with conflict, maladjustment and unhappiness (Wilson, 1965; Miller and Wilson, 1968).

Clinically, we see several patterns of behavior that might truly be considered abnormal by our definition. These are our concern here. A prime example of this is the syndrome associated with a compulsive need to make sexual conquest. When a man exhibits this, it is termed "Don Juanism." The woman is given an equally imaginative but somewhat less romantic label. Depending on precisely how it is manifested, she may be called either a "castrating female" or a "nymphomaniac." We turn first to the male disorder.

The Don Juan, named after the legendary Spanish lover, is a compulsive conqueror of women. He comes only to go, and collects only to recollect. Attraction and capture are his goals; not love. Often, he too suffers from an inadequate self-concept and once capture is successful, he may actually be unable to accept consequent love. The primary sickness, however, is fixation on the initial rewards of a romantic relationship. Don Juan may or may not be fully aware of his goal. Some pursue each relationship with a sincere belief that they are seeking a lasting union. Once achieved, however, they find nothing but disappointment. This response is partly a result of the loss of social reinforcing power suffered by someone once you become secure in the belief that he (or in this case, she) holds a high opinion of you (Aronson and Linden, 1965). Add to this a young man who suffers specific inferiority feelings centering on his social-sexual adequacy and attractiveness, and you have a person who is reinforced exclusively by success in attracting a desirable sexual partner. Of course, since he is insecure in his self-evaluation, he is not convinced of the capture short of sexual surrender. No single success satiates this need. Each time, he finds that he is still left with doubt concerning his attractiveness. He must again prove to himself and to others that he can succeed, almost at will. We hear Don Juan bragging, "I can make any girl I wish." But he doesn't really believe it and he must prove his ability again and again. If success is empty, failure is not. It is filled with terror. Once he commits himself to capture and fails, he must either change his perception of the target's desirability, or face the full impact of his self-doubts. Typically, he thinks in all-or-none fashion. One failure proves he is worthless, one hundred successes, however, fail to convince him that he is worthwhile. The girl he is chasing cannot win, of course. She is damned is she does and damned if she doesn't. Her attractiveness is lowered or lost if she capitulates; she will be viewed as undesirable if she doesn't.

A first cousin to Don Juan is "Marrying Michael." For reasons similar to Juan's, Mike overresponds to the disappointments in marriage described in Chapter IX. However, he is invariably sincere. And marriage is his goal for either moral considerations or because only marriage represents total capture. A sort of serial polygamy results. It is he who contributes so much to the statistics showing an increase in the probability of divorce as the number of previous divorces rises (Landis, 1970).

All of Don Juan's relatives (and they are numerous) appear enviable, happy, and carefree. Most are not. Often, loneliness is the concomitant. Each has learned the need for human contact and intimacy but almost never experiences it. Life is dominated by the drive to demonstrate masculine attractiveness. The motivation to find a lasting and close relationship takes a back seat and rarely directs behavior.

It is only through accident, or the efforts of a most understanding and determined woman, that this poor individual stands any chance of forming a lasting union.

### Wandering Women

The female counterpart of Don Juan probably suffers more social conflict than Juan himself. There still exists (as argued in Chapter VI) a double sexual standard in our culture. Most people still condemn the female libertine. Certainly, sexual conquest is not viewed as an accomplishment for the woman. She is more likely than her male counterpart to be punished for sexual promiscuity, and at the same time she finds weaker social reward. Why then does she ever exhibit this behavior? To answer this question, we must define precisely what behavior we seek to explain. We are interested, here, not in frequent or even varied sexual behavior itself, but in the feminine counterpart of Don Juan. This is the woman who engages in a compulsive serial selection of partners devoid of any true intimacy. Clinical evidence attests that such women do indeed exist. Since controlled research is difficult to conduct in these areas, we must seek answers about causes from these clinical sources. There seems to be a variety of syndromes associated with this behavior. Many of these share elements in common, however. We shall illustrate two variations.

For some of these women, we once again find that low self-esteem and a demanding need for reassurance are prime causal factors. Many girls, caught in the merry-go-round of man seeking, often feel unusually worthless and unable to be truly wanted as human beings. They seem to be saying, "I know you cannot really love me, but you will comfort me a little if you show me that you at least desire my body." What seems surprising at first is that it is often the case that these women were reared under unusually strict and rigid sexual codes. Frequently, they come from supermoral or strictly religious families and, often, they were not allowed to date unchaperoned, or even attend heterosexual parties. They feel as if they had been told: "Sex is bad, and you are bad. We cannot trust you alone with a boy for we know what you are likely to do." Of course, this leaves little room for learning social skills and little opportunity to correct the feelings of worthlessness. Opportunity for potentially corrective early heterosexual contact was too severely limited.

The child has learned that sex is bad, and that, by implication at least, so is she. She has had no chance, in adolescence, to prove her attractiveness to boys. She has been taught that, at the first opportunity, she will indulge in the sin of sex. As an adult, she has the opportunity. And so, of course, she indulges. Why not? It can't make her feel any more strongly immoral. She is already fully convinced of that. Perhaps this is the one thing that she can give of value. It will at least bring someone close for a while. Her low opinion of herself is bound to rub off on her partner. He is likely to develop the same low opinion of her. Thus, it is unlikely that she will be loved, and as we have seen earlier, it is even more unlikely that she will be able to accept love if tendered her. Her interpersonal encounters are usually devoid of any truly mutually enhancing experiences. She moves from one man to another, not so much to conquer as Don Juan does, but in a pitiful plea for love—already completely convinced that, for her, it's unattainable. A sadly self-fulfilling prophecy.

One variant of this type combines the need for sexual reassurance with a rather marked hostility toward men. This peculiar combination usually springs from a combination of training to believe that men are sexually debasing creatures who will use her at every opportunity, and an envy of this power and freedom that men seem to enjoy. Often, too, this girl has actually experienced painful rejection during adolescence or her teenage years. In this case, another kind of motivation enters the picture. She finds some satisfaction in the ability to control and use (perhaps sometimes punish) men through her sexual acts. How powerful she can become by forcing him to please her! How punishing she can be if she lets him know that she gave him the chance but he was unable to satisfy her—damaging his masculinity. Each man that she successfully manipulates in this way (figuratively, "castrates") she can view as weak, impotent, and contemptible. There is little room or opportunity for love in such relationships. It is, in fact, antithetical to her castrating motivations. There is even little room for the enjoyment of sex since enjoying it fully would grant the man success in his masculine endeavor. With so many needs unmet, this woman's behavior fits well our definition of abnormal.

Although the above descriptions in no way exhaust the total possible expressions of Don Juanism, male or female, they serve to illustrate the types of learning experiences that can lead to such a love style.

So far, we have discussed several inabilities to love. There are other variations, most of which, however, are related to the broad types we have described. The purely selfish individual who cares for no one and lives only for his momentary satisfactions, for example, is really another person who failed to form the love-dependence in the early years. The deliberately cruel man who punishes one woman after another is also another Don Juan. He, too, learned fear and hostility toward women. And so it goes. We can usually imagine the learning history from the observed behavior.

An important question, though, is, "If this behavior is learned, can it be unlearned?" That is, can it be cured? While in theory, the answer is a qualified yes, in practice it is not simple. Psychotherapy has demonstrated only limited success. The trouble is, we have no way, as yet, of supplying the cultural learning experiences of infancy once they have been skipped. Our first illness, the total inability to love, seems to be virtually incurable. As for the others, some small success is claimed in treating the faulty self-perceptions underlying much of this behavior. We need, of course, a more rigorous evaluation of our current treatment techniques.

### Jealousy

Jealousy was introduced in Chapter VI. We pointed out that the basis of sexual jealousy in males is found in early childhood experience when the male infant first perceives that some loss of his love object (mother) is caused by the intervention of another, more potent, male (father). As an adult, sexual possession of his female lover by another male reawakens this early shock. Jealousy as an adult is a generalization from the punishing experience of infancy. This is more strongly true for the male than the female. Women, too, form their first love attachments to their mothers. But, when their adult male lovers are attracted to some other female, this does not represent a true reenactment of the early traumatic contest. It is not as compelling a generalization for the female since her mother and her husband are of different sexes.

Most people experience some degree of jealousy. Usually it is not disruptive of the love relationship; in fact, within our culture, jealousy can actually protect or even enhance love. There is, however, a type of demanding, obsessive, and unrealistic jealousy that may deeply threaten or destroy the love relationship. This is not peculiar to the male. Either partner can suffer from it. It is this destructive type of jealousy that concerns us here.

Jealous Jerry's problems were not necessarily apparent at the very beginning of the relationship. When he first met Phyllis he was much taken with her. Jerry overwhelmed her with attention. He gave her little chance to see anyone else because he took up almost all of her free time. He bought her jewelry to make her look "even prettier." He took her to parties to show her off. His obvious pride was very flattering to Phyllis, and before long they were married.

At first, life changed very little. Phyllis, sensitive to exactly how much her looks meant to her husband, took care to show herself only when well groomed. They still went out together often but Jerry was beginning to find himself in a bind. He thoroughly enjoyed exhibiting Phyllis. He wanted and needed to have other men admire her but he was beginning to feel very possessive. The attention she was paid was still pleasing and flattering to him, but it also made him a trifle uneasy. Last time, she was much too pleased when Walt flirted with her. She was encouraging it, wasn't she? Maybe she really *wanted* to make love to him.

Jerry brooded for awhile after that party but said very little to Phyllis about it. Nevertheless, he watched her more closely. Not long after, one night he answered the phone and the party at the other end hung up. Another night, when a tired Phyllis turned down his sexual advances, Jerry blew up. He ranted and raved for hours, accusing Phyllis of every sexual transgression he could think of. He actually didn't believe these accusations and, in fact, they were so extreme that she had no trouble denying and refuting them. They were so absurd, though, that after a short time, Phyllis, who was surprised, hurt, and taken aback, refused to comment on them. The next day, Jerry apologized profusely. He brought Phyllis flowers and castigated himself, admitting that his jealous rage was unwarranted. And he insisted, "I don't know what got into me." However, this was not the end of it. He didn't believe that she had actually done any of the things he had accused her of but he harbored the suspicion that she might want to.

The following week, he came home from work early and Phyllis wasn't there. When she came home (from her girl friend's house), Jerry threw another fit. In four more months they were divorced despite the fact that they really both still loved each other. Why did all of this happen?

Once again, as is so often the case in problems of interpersonal relationship, insecurity and inadequacy feelings played a large part.

Jerry needed the status symbol provided him by a beautiful sex partner because he was not fully convinced that he could really attract
and hold one. His high drive to prove that he could made her beauty
highly reinforcing to him. His doubts about his ability to attract and
keep such a beautiful woman, satisfy and please her, made him highly
sensitive to any evidence that might suggest that she really wasn't
happy with him. It was almost as though the marriage had to break up
to avoid the conflict (in Jerry's perceptions) between his self-doubts
and her satisfaction with him. (See the last section of Chapter VI.) In
the break-up, Jerry actually experiences some relief since he is no longer
required to guard his possession from all of those more attractive
males who would take her away from him, or entertain doubts about
his self-worth.

The type of pathological jealousy we have just illustrated is not
restricted to men, but it is more common in them than in women.
That is not to say that there is any shortage of jealous women. There
are various types of jealousies and some seem to be more frequent
in the female. Let's look at another illustrative example.

Geraldine experienced a somewhat rigid upbringing. She was taught
that "nice girls" love only one man. Sex (with love) was not necessarily bad, but promiscuity was strictly immoral. She dated a lot as a
teenager and enjoyed it immensely. She married young, right after
high school, and lived a relatively pleasant life for the next few years.
Her husband was her only lover, both before and after they were
married. In her early twenties, however, Geraldine began to miss the
fun and the spontaneity of her dating days. She enjoyed flirtations,
but they made her feel guilty and anxious. She found herself constantly in situations where both she and her husband had close contact
with other couples; situations where "switching partners" was not un-
thinkable; in fact, joked about. Soon, she began to harbor jealous
suspicions about her husband. The suspicions turned to accusations;
and they, in turn, to bitter arguments. Once again, the recriminations
snowballed and divorce was the final result.

This type of reaction is called by many names in psychology. Most
commonly, it is termed projection. The mechanism goes like this:
the stimulation of close contact with other men became for Geraldine
a signal with several meanings. It recalled the pleasures of her dating
behavior; it was sexually exciting; it evoked fear and guilt because of
the obvious threat of adultery and the sins of promiscuity that she

had learned to fear. And so, for her own peace of mind, Geraldine sought to avoid thoughts of these intimate contacts; contacts to which she was at least mildly attracted. If she admitted these attractions to herself, she experienced the guilt of immorality that she had been taught was exclusively the province of "fallen women." She could not, in other words, admit to being attracted to other men, or she would necessarily view herself as immoral. She solved the dilemma by avoiding the fear-producing thoughts, while ignoring the reasons. She simply blamed her husband. It was he who was attracted to this new sexual situation. His were the urges to adultery. Some of these urges may or may not have been his. It really doesn't matter. Her jealousy was still unreasonable and disruptive and it destroyed a relationship of mutual love. This type of jealousy, then, is also abnormal.

As pointed out earlier, within the framework of our society, a bit of jealousy (exhibited by both partners, but particularly the male) is expected and, therefore, "normal." Only when it reaches proportions that seriously interfere with an otherwise sound relationship (such as found in the two examples just described) do we consider it pathological. Again, our examples are illustrative and certainly not exhaustive. They are intended to give the reader some insight into what sorts of learning experiences can predispose one to extreme jealousy. There are many different routes to this end. Direct experience with a lover lost to another could surely sensitize anyone to the threat of reoccurrence and, thus, predispose him to jealousy. But whether through fear of comparison, projection, or through direct past experience, an unrealistic and severe jealousy will inevitably destroy love.

So far, we have discussed reactions that disrupt the ability to form or maintain love relationships. It is also true that disorders of the love relationship can affect related behavior to a marked degree. The interaction of love and sex is a prime example of this. Many of the so-called sexual disorders are in part secondary to some primary disturbance of the love interaction. We shall turn to some of these now.

## Problems of Sexual Functioning

Our sexual responses are physiological functions that are aroused by physical and psychological stimuli. In brief, the aroused male will experience physiological excitation, mediated largely by the autonomic nervous system. His blood pressure and pulse will rise; his muscles will increase in tension; his skin will blush; and he will experience tumescence or penile erection. If adequate sexual stimulation continues, his excitement will increase; involuntary thrusting movements of the pelvis will occur and increase; many muscle groups will tense further; and he will experience orgasm and seminal fluid ejaculation, followed by a fairly rapid decrease in muscular and psychological tension.

The sexually stimulated human female undergoes much the same sequence of events, but with several significant differences. Vaginal lubrication occurs early in excitation; the vaginal lips spread and change color; tumescence is primarily of the erectile tissue of the clitoris and, secondarily, of the nipples of the breast; there is no ejaculation with orgasm; the orgasmic phase is often prolonged with repeated orgasms possible under continued stimulation; and the resolution phase is usually somewhat slower.

In both sexes, the normal course of sexual behavior may suffer interference in several ways. It can be disrupted by biological dysfunction, through disease, age, drugs, or through psychological aberration. Except for aging (the biological effects of which are far less severe on sex than most of us believe), physiological dysfunction is usually obvious and relatively uncommon. Our concern here is with psychological breakdown, particularly with problems that relate directly to the relationship between the two partners.

For various psychological reasons, the male, once aroused, may fail to achieve or maintain an erection (impotence), may ejaculate too early to accomplish successful intercourse (premature ejaculation), or may fail to ejaculate intravaginally at all (ejaculatory incompetence). The female may experience spasms of her vaginal muscles and thus deny penile entry (vaginismus), may experience intense pain with intercourse (dyspareunia), or may fail to lubricate or experience orgasm (commonly, "frigidity"). Any or all of these blocks to successful intercourse can occur, in either sex, in spite of the conscious and expressed wishes of the sufferer. Why?

It is easy to refer to conflicting motivations and to blame sexual disability on "inhibitions." It is even simple to identify and name possible conflicts. But it is a far more difficult task to describe a mechanism whereby conflicting motivations can, in fact, interfere with sexual ability. The answer to this last and central issue is found in an understanding of sexual stimulation, applying once again our principles of learning.

Just what constitutes adequate sexual stimulation is a complicated question. The phrase "physical and psychological stimulation" is a common catch-all evasion that is most difficult to spell out. In analyzing its meaning, we shall start with a definition that may appear circular at first: Adequate sexual stimulation is that pattern of stimuli which results in sexual excitation.

Throughout the animal kingdom, we find that there are stimuli that innately release patterns of sexual response (Eibl-Eibesfeldt, 1970). These are "species specific," that is, different for different kinds of animals. In addition to evolved, specific, inborn responses to stimuli, experience, that is, learning, plays a great part in what produces sexual excitation. Thus there are vast differences in what is sexually arousing to different organisms. Smell is an important ingredient of the stimulus complex for many infrahuman mammals; sound for many insects and birds; sight and taste for fish; and, among other things, sight, sound, touch, and complicated imagery in humans. Apparently there are wide differences among individuals also, at least as far as humans are concerned. Clearly we are turned on sexually by different things. Tastes vary, and what is adequate sexual stimulation for one individual, may bore or offend another. So, if the stimuli for arousal differ, the causes of arousal disorder must also vary somewhat. Nevertheless, most of them are related to interference, in some way, with receiving the signals. Cats that can't smell, and crickets that can't hear, will surely be sexually handicapped. Similarly, human beings who experience a block of full feel and imagery of sexual stimulation will consequently suffer a decrease in sexual responsiveness. Masters and Johnson (1970) describe several such sensory blocks, as they relate to the specific clinical entities of sexual dysfunction. Their writings constitute, to date, the most reliable source of information, and a significant portion of the discussion that follows draws on their findings.

As human beings, we are sexually excited, or are readied for intercourse, by direct stimulation of our senses from "sexual" stimuli, and by "indirect" stimuli arising from our perception of an aroused partner. For convenience, we shall arbitrarily classify these stimuli as physical and psychological respectively. This distinction is blurred, however, since both types of stimuli (direct or indirect) are dependent both on physical events and on our psychological interpretation of these events. The point is that both classes of exciting stimuli may be blocked, or can be avoided, either physically or psychologically. We feel our skin stroked; we hear and see our naked partners. We also experience or sense the partner's excitement as desire builds. These stimuli arouse and ready us for intercourse. Our sexual responses become automatic or involuntary. We cannot and need not "will" erection, vaginal lubrication, or orgasms. They simply occur. If we attempt to will these responses, it only hinders our reception of the arousing stimuli.

Daily, we practice avoiding sexual stimuli. Of our biological drives, sex is extreme in the amount of effort we spend inhibiting it. It is inappropriate to get sexually excited when brushing against an attractive stranger in an elevator and so we learn to avoid the exact stimuli and the perceptions that cause this. We learn to inhibit sexual response partly through avoiding the stimuli. Some of us, because of religious, moral, or other social conflicts, may learn too well. Sexual responsiveness becomes almost totally inhibited. In any case, the mechanisms for turning ourselves off sexually are available to us and can be brought into play even when we do not consciously desire the inhibitory outcome. Thus we have the sexual aberrations and inadequacies described earlier in this chapter.

Obviously, if we consciously desire sexual relations and our bodies do not respond, we are in conflict. Not only is conflict a result of this nonresponsiveness but it is also frequently the cause. We avoid stimuli that threaten punishment, and there are many ways in which the intensely interpersonal encounter of sex can make us feel fear of punishment. When this occurs, our anxieties lead us away from easy receptivity to sexual stimuli, and we suffer some degree of sexual dysfunction. Let us illustrate some of the possible ways through which ambivalence and anxiety can cause such interference.

### Fear of Inadequacy

Just how we view ourselves usually determines how we behave. If our self-views are faulty, our behavior will be ineffective in proportion to the distortion. In the realm of sex, faulty self-perception, particularly the sense of inadequacy, is so prevalent that Masters and Johnson (1970, pp. 12–13) have commented:

"It should be restated that fear of inadequacy is the greatest known deterrent to effective sexual functioning, simply because it so completely distracts the fearful individual from his or her natural responsivity by blocking reception of sexual stimuli either created by or reflected from the sexual partner."

This fear of inadequacy can lead to what Masters and Johnson (1970) term the "spectator" syndrome; concern with performance leads one or both partners to watch intensely for signs of sexual inadequacy rather than simply allowing the signals of erotic encounter to lead naturally to sexuality. If worried about erection, or his lover's response, the male is, in effect, distracted. He is more an observer or spectator than a participant. The same affliction can strike the woman. Under many circumstances, she too may watch the game more than play it. Sex, of course, was not really designed to be a spectator sport.

Whether one or both partners suffer from this disturbance to an extent sufficient to cause pathological symptoms is almost irrelevant. As much as the individual, it is the love relationship itself that is impaired. If we fear inadequacy, we are obviously anxious about our partner's reactions. The fear bespeaks a lack of communication and trust that must be blamed on the relationship itself. Whether or not the partner is really highly critical, the fact that we fear this possibility is indicative of a flaw in the interaction that can be corrected only by improving the total relationship. The treatment of sexual disorders, whatever the type of therapy, is far more successful when both partners are involved and the therapy is directed toward the relationship. Let's illustrate with a fictional but plausible case.

Duane was a college graduate who had become a junior executive with a large corporation. At thirty, he was successful professionally and had been married for four years to Janet, a woman who worked for the same firm. They had one daughter.

Duane had an uneventful childhood with no sexual trauma. Prior to his marriage, he had dated a moderate amount and had experienced two sexual affairs wherein he was the aggressor and seduced rather shy and inexperienced women. His wife, however, was sexually aggressive, experienced, and sophisticated. Although they truly loved each other, Duane was slightly awed by Janet's superior sexual knowledge. Nevertheless, they lived together, in and out of bed, with a reasonable degree of happiness and no serious problems. Then one night, after drinking excessively at a party, Janet aggressively instigated sex play. Duane was tired and drunk, but fearing to disappoint her, he gamely attempted to make love. He failed through impotence. Humiliated and frustrated, they both went to sleep.

The next day, while hung over, Duane suffered nagging anxiety that he was unable to pinpoint. But that night, in bed, the reason for his fears became distressingly clear. He had failed the night before. And what if it should happen again? He waited and watched. They engaged in the old familiar routines and, finally, with feelings of deep relief, successfully made love. But the pattern of anxiety had been established; two spectators had been born. Later, for little apparent reason, Duane found himself once again impotent. And the frequency of such occurrences increased. Soon Janet also became anxious; so anxious that her responsivity was hampered. Sex became infrequent and tension-filled.

This is a case of what is termed secondary impotence (it would have been primary had Duane never exhibited the ability to achieve a normal erection). It is not uncommon. Many men, perhaps most, experience episodes of partial or total impotence at one time or another in their lives. Alcohol, distractions, worries, or even simple fatigue, can cause this. It becomes a problem only when, as with Duane, it causes so much anxiety in the situation that the participant becomes an involuntary spectator to his own lovemaking efforts. He had always been a little uneasy about his sexual adequacy in relation to Janet. How did he compare with her previous lovers? Was his relative inexperience distressing to her? And, somehow, Janet had never offered reassurance sufficient to calm his anxiety.

It should be emphasized that anxiety which was the final result of self-doubt ultimately led to the problem of impotence. Anxiety involves a heightened autonomic nervous system reaction, particularly the sympathetic branch. It has long been noted that anxiety interferes with sexual functioning. And now there is physiological evidence to support this observation. Sympathetic stimulation apparently controls ejaculation but arousal and all that goes with it (tumescence, etc.) are probably controlled by the parasympathetic system (Zuckerman 1971). Since there is some antagonism of function between the sympathetic and parasympathetic branches of the autonomic nervous system, excessive sympathetic activity, brought on by anxiety, could interfere with arousal and cause both impotence and premature ejaculation in the male along with orgasmic problems and dyspareunia in the female. This physiological mechanism for interfering with sexual function can certainly be influenced by learning. Not only is anxiety learned, it is also potentially unlearned, or extinguished through therapy. Neurotic needs can be served by unconsciously learning to use these mechanisms in order to avoid successful sex. This, too, can be unlearned.

In treatment, the entire relationship must be examined. It must be discovered whether either one or the other of the couple in some way wants to avoid sex. If so, the reasons must be found and confronted. Whatever the reason, treatment can usually be instituted to slowly extinguish anxieties that have built up around the sexual situation. The method of extinction that seems best suited to these circumstances is basically one called "toleration." The feared stimulus is introduced a little at a time, under controlled circumstances, in ever increasing doses until its full impact can be safely experienced with no punishing or fearful effects.

Of course, the basis for the fear must be removed. False assumptions about each other's demands and simple misinformation about sexual functioning often contribute to sexual anxieties. Discussion of these matters with an authority can help dispel these notions. Moreover, talking about them is, itself, a step toward extinguishing anxiety, for words stand for the actual stimuli. Words possess some of the power to evoke the same responses; in this case, anxiety (see Chapter II). After diagnostic and therapeutic discussions, the couple is usually instructed to experiment with sex slowly under nondemanding circumstances but with ever-increasing frequency. A full discussion of one excellent way in which this type of treatment is used is found in Masters and Johnson (1970).

Duane and Janet's experience is typical of the way in which fear of inadequacy can build to destructive sexual anxiety. Duane's self-perceptions had never been too flattering. His past experience was confined to situations that he controlled fully, wherein he played the role of the aggressive, relatively more experienced partner. Janet's greater experience and self-confidence threatened him and eventually contributed heavily to the problem. In extreme cases, the fear of inadequacy can lead to primary impotence, ejaculatory incompetence, and occasionally, premature ejaculation in the male, or dyspareunia (due usually to inadequate lubrication), vaginismus, or frigidity in the female. These (and other sexual disorders) also have other causes. Let's explore some of these.

*Guilt*

Probably the second most frequent cause of sexual dysfunction is guilt, or more generally, some vague expectation of punishment for sexual behavior. The "sex-is-bad" attitude (Chapter VI) that still lingers in our society may be acquired directly through religious or so-called moral training, or may be learned more subtly through indirect social approval or disapproval. For example, without ever actually stating a negative attitude, parents may teach their children to feel that sex is wrong by simply approving conservative television programs, movies, clothing styles, and language, while disapproving more liberal expression in these areas. This type of attitude training is difficult to combat because it usually takes the form of vague feelings rather than words, and it covers a wide range of situations and behaviors. To the extent that we have learned these attitudes about sex, we feel uncomfortable and guilty in sexual situations. If the discomfort is severe enough, sex is avoided altogether. If the desire for sex is strong, there results a paralyzing conflict that makes full sexual enjoyment impossible.

When guilt acts simply as a distraction, it can result in a state highly similar to that just described in fear of inadequacy. Not uncommonly, however, we actually learn active (or passive) mechanisms that make sexual contacts impossible, and thus we relieve the guilt and avoid vague anticipated punishment. Vaginismus is an example of this. The frightened female may learn unconsciously that entry of her vagina can be blocked by a muscle spasm that closes the vaginal canal. She may be unaware of anything other than the fact that she cannot have intercourse and will even likely verbalize a desire to do so. Nevertheless, she has learned an effective unconscious mechanism for avoiding the frightening aspects of sex while still maintaining intellectual consistency with an "enlightened" attitude. Both partners are so frequently unaware of precisely what the problem is that many cases of vaginismus are discovered "accidentally" by a surprised gynecologist during an attempted pelvic examination.

In one way or another, the distractions of conflict or guilt can cause most of the sexual dysfunctions we have mentioned. Premature ejaculation (although also caused by other problems) can quickly remove one from an anxious, guilty situation. As a result, the love relationship suffers not only from the loss of sex but also from the real or fancied rejection that this represents to the partner. In most cases, the most effective treatment is the same as that described above for fear of inadequacy. The attitude must be changed through extinction of the fear-guilt reaction. The probability of successful treatment, given a cooperative couple, is high. Modern treatment programs report 80 percent or better success.

## Hostility and Rejection

A third important cause of sexual problems is one that arises directly from the relationship between the partners. We are talking about a broad group of difficulties with more potential variation than there are couples. But we shall discuss some important general problem areas that are common to many different specific situations.

It is often said that enjoyable sex is an expression of a good love relationship, and that most troubles do not start in the bedroom but are merely felt there. This is only partly true, but that part is important. A good relationship is no guarantee of good sex. But a bad relationship is usually associated with at least some degree of sexual dysfunction. Erotic intimacy presents an unparalleled opportunity to express and communicate many things—from love, respect, and desire, to hostility, rejection, and hatred.

Again, dysfunction has multiple causes. Some disorders, however, are more frequently associated with certain types of problems than with others. One illustration is the possible effect of marital hostility on male ejaculatory competence. Although ejaculatory incompetence may spring from the spectator syndrome (anxiety), it may be caused also by an unconsciously learned mechanism. Withholding the orgasm expresses hostility. Most men learn the techniques of ejaculatory control (usually simple deliberate self-distraction) as a mechanism for prolonging intercourse (or avoiding pregnancy). This mechanism can readily serve hostility or rejection. The husband who has never accepted his marriage, for example, may fail, symbolically, to consummate it by not ejaculating intravaginally. This results, of course, in a withholding of pleasure from both partners, and frequently communicates a clear message of rejection.

Related in some ways to ejaculatory incompetence, is premature ejaculation. Although usually the result of simple inexperience and anxiety (see above), hostility can be involved. If the male ends the sexual contact prematurely (before his partner can attain orgasm), he could very well be expressing indifference or hostility toward his partner. Sometimes, premature ejaculation of the male also relieves the woman's fears of sex. Both she and her lover may suffer from the attitude that free female acceptance of sexual pleasure is sinful. And so neither of them really wants to change the established pattern. Often, these motivations are present in some combination in both partners, and so, once again, it is the relationship that must be examined, not the individual.

In general, any failure to respond fully in a sexual situation can be caused by hostility or rejection. The wife who merely tolerates her husband's sexual advances may be telling him that he does not excite her or, perhaps, may be even punishing him for some real or fancied wrong he has committed. It should be emphasized, however, that while most cases of sexual dysfunction are not caused primarily by hostility, they may eventually lead to this as the relationship deteriorates. Recalling that one of the major sources of sexual stimulation is the response of the partner, it is clear that any sexual inadequacy will affect both partners whether or not it is caused originally by an interpersonal problem. Each relationship leads to different problems and to different sexual "messages." Ways of using sexual intimacy as a reward or a punishment, as well as an expression of the deepest need, are almost without limit.

Although degree of sex drive varies from person to person, a compatible couple can usually arrive at a workable compromise on frequency of contact. It is unnecessary for both partners to be at the peak of sexual excitement each time they make love. Under many circumstances, the pleasure of simply accommodating the other's desire is a sufficiently rewarding experience for lovemaking to go smoothly. But some degree of mutual acceptance is the key. Both unnecessary denial of sex and unreasonable demand can be used by either partner to test the other or to express hostility. Constant disagreement over frequency is, then, as much as anything else, a signal of love awry. Sex should be a joy to both participants. Whenever any aspect of sex becomes aversive or painful to either partner, this is a sign that something is wrong in the relationship. Trouble already exists, or soon will.

An area of major importance in what may be called abnormal love (or sex) is homosexuality (usually termed lesbianism when applied to females). This issue deserves a close look.

SUGGESTED READING

Masters, W. H., & Johnson, V. E. *Human sexual inadequacy.* Boston: Little, Brown, 1970.

# CHAPTER XIII

# Homosexuality

SUMMARY

Our society deals harshly with homosexuality. It is viewed as un-natural, immoral, even criminal. In no meaningful sense can it be called unnatural, since it develops in accordance with the laws of nature, and most mammals and many human societies throughout history have practiced it freely. Immorality is a slippery concept to define, and illegality is not inherent in the act but rather in the re-sponse to it made by our culture. In spite of the legal and social sanc-tions, homosexuality, in both the male and female, is quite prevalent in our country, with literally millions of practitioners.

Unquestionably, both biological and social factors contribute to our sexual preferences. There are many different types of homosexuality and many different directions taken by each of these types. The homo-sexual's love for his partner can be a true love, developing in accor-dance with the principles of learning that account for any other type of love. The potential rewards in the relationships are manifold.

In view of the frequency of homosexuality, and its basically in-nocuous nature, perhaps the officially rigid values our society holds against it should be reexamined.

It is common, normal, and usually desirable, for men to love men and women to love women, but the exact circumstances governing the expression of that love are quite restrictive. Breach of this code changes friendship to homosexuality. Our society condones the in-timate rewards of sex under very limited conditions. One of the most stringent of these conditions is the insistence on heterosexuality. Most of us believe that this is the way "intended by nature" and thus,

153

"natural." It is argued that sex is a prelude to procreation and, since homosexual procreation is impossible, it follows that homosexual sex is unnatural. If we are going to be consistent, this argument should apply equally strongly to any sexual contact that employs contraception. It is also held that other animals have no homosexual contacts, but this is entirely false; homosexual activity is widespread throughout the mammalian kingdom, both as mammalian prepubescent play and even among adult animals (Dobzhansky, 1962).

The list of reasons cited in condemnation of homosexuality is long and mostly false. They all lead to the same conclusion: homosexuality is unnatural, abnormal, immoral, and sick.

Not all societies feel that way, and there is evidence that even ours is softening somewhat in this attitude (see, for example, Trainer, 1970). But our antihomosexual value system still runs strong and deep, influencing all of us in the ways in which we respond to our own sexuality, whether heterosexual or homosexual. Love relationships of all sorts are affected by the threat of the taint of homosexuality. Men often go out of their way to prove their virility and their heterosexual nature partly just to guard against the accusation that they might be inclined otherwise. Women, too, often suffer from a form of homosexual anxiety that directs their behaviors toward uncomfortable and artificial extremes. Let us try to understand this phenomenon by looking further into the nature of sex roles and sexual attraction.

We begin to learn appropriate sex roles in early childhood. We learn how boys behave and how girls behave, the sometimes small but always significant differences in play, in dress, in speech, in mannerisms, and in tastes. We are well tutored in the male-female distinction long before we gain any real understanding of sex. We learn which role is expected of us and we are impelled in that direction. In view of the severe social punishment suffered by anyone who fails to play his proper role, it is really rather surprising that homosexuality, or any sort of role inversion, has any appreciable frequency at all. But it does; Kinsey, Pomeroy, and Martin (1948) found that 37 percent of the postpuberal male population admitted at least one full homosexual contact, and that 4 percent admitted to being exclusively homosexual. Accuracy of count with respect to this issue is obviously hard to come by, for verbal reports in such areas are, of course, not wholly reliable. And if we include sexual contacts that do not end in orgasm, the incidence runs even higher. It is surely not rare.

In a very real sense, we are all bisexual. That is, physically, we are capable of being sexually stimulated by contacts with either sex (or, for that matter, even by mechanical means). Yet only a very small minority of us are truly psychologically bisexual; that is, most of us exhibit a strong preference for one sex. What determines this preference? Are we born with it? Do we learn it? Or is it some combination of these two?

This question is a live one. The answer, elusive as it may be, casts light upon where we must look for an understanding of most of our lives. The nature-nurture question, however, is now phrased in a more complex and sophisticated manner than when it was merely asked whether a given trait was inherited or acquired. Human behavior is no longer viewed as that simple. We all learn within the framework of biological structure, which, in turn, develops within an environment. So, heredity and environment are not fully separable entities, but rather two interacting aspects of development. It is meaningful, however, to ask what proportion of trait differences in a given group of people is attributable to different genetic endowments, and what proportion to different environments. Thus, we have the concept of heritability (a more technical definition of which is beyond the scope of this book) which applies to sexual preference as well as all other human characteristics.

Some investigators have considered heredity a major determinant of homosexual behavior (e.g., Kallman, 1952, 1953) but because of many obvious difficulties in such studies, the precise percentage of heritability of homosexuality has not yet been fully established. At least, though, the complicated interaction of biology and psychology that produces it is becoming a little clearer. Our present state of knowledge, however, suggests that, in practical terms, there is a more immediately important question. We need to define, quite clearly, the behavior with which we are concerned before we can assess the relative importance of various causes. There is a wide range of behavior that can be labeled homosexual, from people who have always exhibited an exclusively homosexual preference (chronic, obligative) to those who may have expressed only a limited homosexual outlet experienced in a single homosexual seduction. The best review of this issue, to date, is that of Money (1970), who writes: (p. 425)

"Whatever the degree of an individual's homosexual commitment, the behavior concerned may be in some degree hereditary, constitutional and biological in its determination, and in some degree environmental, learned, and sociological. It is not a question of either/or with respect to each of these categories, or a question of how much; the basic question is, which type? The chronic and obligative, essential or idiopathic homosexual, may be a product of the confluence of heredity and environment, constitution and learning, biology and sociology. Likewise, with the transitory, facultative, optional, and induced homosexual."

Money then adds a footnote: "Exactly the same statements may be made of the heterosexual."

To understand homosexuality, we must gain some understanding of the wider issue of sexual preference in general since individual choice covers the entire range from exclusively heterosexual to exclusively homosexual behavior, and there seems to be no clear dividing line. Moreover, if there are many varieties of behavior, there is even wider variety in the causes of these behaviors, with both hormones and histories interacting in all of them.

In the course of normal fetal differentiation, both sexes first develop the female sexual organs. The formation of male sexual characteristics requires the presence of androgens (male sex hormones) *in utero*. If these androgens are absent, or, if their action is somehow blocked (which is chemically possible), then the embryo will develop morphologically as female regardless of its genetic constitution. If these androgens are present during the critical developmental period, then male sex organs will develop, again, regardless of the embryo's genetic constitution. Because of physiologic dysfunction, there are a number of known cases of sexual disagreement between the genes and physical sex characteristics, in both directions. That is, there are some genetic females (carrying the female XX chromosomes) who are anatomically male; there are also some known cases of genetic males (XY chromosomes) who are morphologically female (Money, 1970). A study of these people and their psychosexual development sheds light on the factors shaping sex preference.

It is a striking fact, seen in the histories of these and other endocrine cases, that neither genes nor hormones are sufficient to automatically produce sexual preference by themselves. The same can be said of body morphology. The presence or absence of accurate amounts of androgen during fetal development unquestionably influences aggressiveness and probably, tastes and behavior in general. But in the absence of the life experiences, this factor is not sufficient to direct sexual preference. It has been noted recently (Kalodny, et al., 1971) that androgen levels (specifically testosterone) seem to be lower in predominantly homosexual as opposed to heterosexual males. The cause, however, is still unclear and surely not simple. In other words, although homosexuality may be due, in part, to a predisposition toward the values of the "wrong" sex because of a prenatal (or even later) hormone problem, the homosexual identity is still also determined partially by the social circumstances which somehow teach this sex role. We still must learn the sexual role. How do these learning experiences lead us to a psychosexual identity?

As pointed out earlier, simply growing up in our society usually provides plentiful opportunities to learn the differences in the behaviors of males and females. In addition to observation and modeling, we are quite directly shaped in our actions. Usually, the boy is rewarded by his family and his peers for expressing male mannerisms and interests, while he is punished through ridicule (at the very least) for expressing feminine ones. The same principles hold for the female, but to a somewhat lesser extent (which just might bear some relationship to the recent interest in unisex and in women's liberation movements). The rewards for maintaining "proper" sex identity continue, generally, through adolescence and adulthood. Our social system is geared to the heterosexual couple; and heterosexual attachments are rewarded both within the relationship and without. So the learning bias is firmly established in our society (given a normal family structure). We are taught the appropriate actions of one sex and these include sexual and emotional attraction to the opposite sex. But, as literally millions of "sexual misfits" in our society can well attest, it doesn't always work out. There are many ways in which the accepted normal course of psychosexual development can go awry. We shall look at some of the "accidents" that can happen. First, we shall explore the misplaced masculinity of the male, men who turn to other men for sexual release.

## Male Homosexuality

As a class, manly behaviors are somewhat more physical and aggressive than are typical feminine pursuits. Rough and tumble play in childhood, and the stronger expression of overt hostility in adulthood, characterize masculinity as opposed to femininity. This is not entirely a cultural accident. To some extent, our needs heed our hormones, and androgens seem to be correlated with aggressiveness. So, for most men in our society, there is a biological leaning toward acceptance of the masculine interest in addition to the social pressures to do so.

One of these masculine interests, obviously a prime one, is a sexual attraction to women. This preference is separable from the entire complex of masculinity. That is, some men with homosexual preferences exhibit an otherwise masculine set of interests, and others, a relatively feminine set. This distinction frequently (but not always) corresponds to taking the active (masculine) or passive (feminine) role in sexual contacts. It is an unproved, but at least superficially attractive hypothesis that genetic predisposition plays some part in determining general masculinity. On the other hand, it seems virtually certain that it is not the only factor involved.

It is impossible in this brief space to do justice to the almost infinite number of behavior routes that our sexual preferences can take. And so, we shall attempt only to illustrate how a few factors and experiences might lead to homosexuality. Let us, again, use the device of the fictional case history.

### "Queen" Eric

Eric's mother was domineering and hostile. His father was not only quiet and submissive but also frequently physically absent from the home because of his job. As a consequence, Eric was reared almost exclusively by his mother together with her sister who lived with them. To exaggerate the situation, his parents were divorced when he was six years old, and from then on, he was reared totally by the two women. One study (Thomas, 1968), has shown that children reared in homes without men attribute more duties to the female in their learning of sex roles than do children reared with both parents present. Thus Eric might come to believe that his assumption of normal tasks made him feminine. Moreover, both women were bitter about men. It seemed that everything men did or stood for was pretty much regarded as bad by these two most important people in Eric's life. He soon learned that the only way he could gain their approval was to act in as unmasculine a manner as possible. In other words, Eric's rewarding experiences were reversed; feminine behavior was rewarded by approval, and masculine behavior was punished by disapproval. Consequently, he took on the feminine role.

Part of what Eric learned was the attitude that men take advantage of women by using them sexually, and that this is indeed bad. At the same time, he developed (through directly observing this behavior in his conflicted mother and aunt) some fascination for being sexually "used." He was sure that he didn't want to use women sexually, but he was not quite so sure that he didn't want to experience being used himself.

The remainder of Eric's story is straightforward. He had a great deal of difficulty making friends. His effeminacy helped produce almost total ostracism by his peers. Finally, an older confirmed homosexual befriended him, providing Eric with acceptance, rewarding companionship and, eventually, love. In gratitude and curiosity, Eric allowed his friend to provide for him and derive from him sexual pleasure. Thus, the elements of a true (but homosexual) love affair were all present. And Eric learned not only to love this man but also to become a homosexual.

It is interesting to note in Eric's case, that he not only became a confirmed homosexual, but he manifested a distinctly female role (as he learned it) both generally and sexually. Nevertheless, it is unnecessary to assume a glandular predisposition toward femininity. Perhaps it was present, and it could have helped him adopt the role, but this factor is by no means a requirement for such behavior. It is also important to take note of the fact that Eric's homosexual romance possessed all of the elements of heterosexual love. In the subculture in which he eventually found himself, attraction, infatuation, jealousy, and virtually all of the other phenomena of heterosexual love were present.

Other, quite different paths can also lead to homosexuality. Let us illustrate another.

*Tom—The Masculine Homosexual*

Tom was not a particularly attractive child, but he was well built and masculine looking. Both parents were living but he was not especially close to either. He was reinforced for, and exhibited, the masculine traits expected of him. He was, however, a little more insecure than most children, never feeling quite sure that his parents loved him, and rather strongly convinced that most of his friends did not. It was particularly in his relation to females that he felt the greatest inadequacy, although it became increasingly important to him to be accepted and liked by both sexes.

In adolescence, Tom experienced a high level of sexual tension. He discovered masturbation early and used it frequently. Usually this was accompanied by some fantasy of heterosexual conquest. Tom's male friends were very important to him, and although he was relatively domineering and aggressive with them, he remained shy with girls. Eventually, his need to be loved and accepted by his friends became entwined with his high sex drive. He and his best buddy began to experiment with mutual masturbation. It frightened both of them at first, but it also drew them closer together because it represented shared and forbidden pleasure. Tom's dominance in the relationship asserted itself, and soon they had a full-blown homosexual affair wherein Tom assumed the more masculine role. Thereafter, Tom sought sexual release primarily through homosexual contacts during which he always played the masculine role. His lovers were actually substitute women. He chose this route because he found it easier to approach men than women.

People like Tom often also function heterosexually when nonthreatening opportunities present themselves. Usually, however, they maintain a preference for males because of greater security in that situation. It is again worth noting that biology surely did not cause Tom's homosexual behavior except, of course, in the very indirect sense of producing a strong (yet undirected) sex drive.

It should be reemphasized that relationships such as Tom's and Eric's often represent real and intense love. In spite of all of the handicaps and hardships experienced by a homosexual couple in our predominantly heterosexual culture, there are some genuine advantages. The shared values, for example, of two homosexual males (and, therefore, the opportunity for shared pleasures) are likely to be much more nearly similar than the values of heterosexual couples. Nevertheless, most homosexuals in our society lead anxious and unhappy lives filled with conflict. This is not true in some other cultures that have adopted a more accepting role.

Let us turn now from these brief illustrations of some possible mechanisms in male homosexuality to a consideration of lesbianism.

### Lesbianism

Based in part on the Kinsey studies (see Chapter VI and above), it is a commonly held belief that lesbianism is less frequent than male homosexuality, but there is reason to question this. Frequency comparisons are difficult to make for standards used to define homosexuality are not the same in women as in men. Although Kinsey, Pomeroy, and Martin (1949, 1953) found that only 28 percent of all the females in their sample admitted to having lesbian experiences (as opposed to 50 percent of the males), it is entirely possible that there is some difference in willingness to admit to such experiences. But more important is the fact that more interfemale expression of affection is expected and accepted than intermale. Kissing and hugging among women is far more common than men, and rarely suggests lesbianism to the observer. Furthermore, lesbianism, when it does occur, is taken much less seriously than male homosexuality. Ford and Beach (1951, p. 126) write:

"The attitude of our society toward feminine homosexuality might almost be characterized as one of disregard. The legal codes of many states provide severe penalties for men convicted of homosexual practices, but very few states have similar laws pertaining to women. Katherine David interprets this discrepancy as a reflection of the fact that intimacies between women tend to be taken for granted. She adds that feminine inversion differs from masculine homosexuality in being more closely associated with sentiments and emotions that transcend a purely physical attraction."

In other words, lesbianism may be counted as rarer than male homosexuality because, in some forms, it is so common that it is not viewed as abnormal! Out of 295 women interviewed by Landis et al. (1940), 273 reported having experienced "strong libidinal attachment to members of their own sex." While we certainly cannot conclude that all of these are truly what we might term lesbian contacts, it is most assuredly suggestive (at least) that women-to-women love attachments are very common, indeed. This should not be surprising.

It has been pointed out repeatedly in this book, that most of us learn love first through experiences with our mothers. This early and powerful love is experienced by women as well as men. It is tempting, then, to suggest that women should find it easy to generalize this early love to another female later on. The frequency with which this love is expressed physically in overt sexual acts is open to question. The very criteria for labeling lesbianism are ill defined. Physical contact to orgasm is not as simple a criterion in women as in men since the frequency of orgasm in women is substantially lower than that in men. Aside from questions of frequency, we have the more important issue of what leads women to select other women as major or exclusive sources of sexual stimulation and gratification. In a society where we are taught that our sexual contacts should be between sexes, not within, we must explain why some women display sexual preferences that oppose this teaching. Why is heterosexual social training effective in the case of one woman, but not in another? Again, as with male homosexuality, we shall suggest some broad possible reasons.

### Fear of Men

Strangely enough, upbringing remarkably similar to Eric's can lead to lesbianism when experienced by a female. For example, Liz, also the product of an unhappy and eventually broken marriage, remained with her mother after her divorce. Her mother took on a female boarder to help meet expenses. Both of these ladies had suffered bad experiences with men, and both frequently expressed the feeling that they had been used and abused by man. Fearing that Liz would also become some man's mere sexual toy, they took care to teach her the evils of sex. Liz was taught that men were cruel, crude, physically abusive, and uncaring. She was also encouraged to believe that the physical sex act was painful and frightening. Men were dirty and disgusting. Liz learned well. In spite of the many heterosexual activities that went on about her at school, activities that were apparently enjoyed by her female friends, she felt only disgust and discomfort around males.

For expressing a sexually prudish attitude and for not dating, Liz was well reinforced by the approval and love (frequently physically expressed as kissing and hugging) of her mother and mother's boarder. This affection was her major source of social reward and she became very dependent on it. One night, in her mother's absence, the boarder went a bit further than usual in displaying affection by fondling Liz's body, only lightly and playfully, but clearly. Liz was confused, but the affection and the physical pleasure were both rewarding to her, and so, she did not protest. Later, the game developed further and Liz learned the pleasures of sex in a homosexual setting. And so, she relieved her fears, gained a strong affectional relationship, and became capable of enjoying sex, all at the same time. For Liz, lesbianism became the answer to her sexual-social dilemma.

Fear of men is only one of many possible causes of lesbianism. There are undoubtedly as many pathways to lesbianism as to male homosexuality. Biology plays a part as well as learning. Excessively androgenic females acquire masculine interests and characteristics which may make it easier for them to take on a masculine psychosexual identification when exposed to certain learning experiences. But the relative contribution of this biological factor is quite unknown (Money, 1970). We can only say that sexual preference, as in most behavior, is shaped by biology as well as rewards and punishments. And that both male and female homosexuals are typically rewarded for homosexual behavior and usually punished for heterosexual acts.

The high incidence of homosexual contacts, suggests that we either make the heterosexual experience quite aversive for a lot of people or the intrinsic rewards of homosexuality are very great. Perhaps both. In any case, whatever its causes, whatever its incidence, and however we choose to view it, homosexual love is often love in the true sense of the word. Two people of the same sex can (and often do) provide many rewards for each other, socially, emotionally, and physically. Our society condemns this relationship and, in so doing, makes life quite difficult for the person who chooses to take the homosexual route. We can only speculate that society's condemnation may have developed out of the fear that such a relationship threatens our basic family-child oriented pattern. Our growing overpopulation crisis recommends that these values be reexamined. Furthermore, homosexuality is obviously a part of our culture, and it seems almost absurd to brand such people criminal for acts that, in the final analysis, are quite harmless when carried out between consenting adults.

SUGGESTED READING

Maccoby, E. E. (Ed.) *The development of sex differences.* Stanford, California: Stanford Univ. Press, 1966.

Money, J. Sexual dimorphism and homosexual gender identity. *Psychological Bulletin*, 1970, 74, 425–440.

# CHAPTER XIV

# Conceptions and Directions

## SUMMARY

Losing the feeling of missing a lost lover is somewhat different from extinguishing love itself. It is difficult to extinguish a response to an absent stimulus. However, we can eventually extinguish the expectation that our lost lover will be there to reward us. This describes the mending of a broken heart. Actively seeking other sources of rewards, and other people to bring them about and with whom we can share them, is an effective mechanism in recovering from a lost love.

Love and hate share two common features. They are both broad, general responses to human beings (approach and avoidance, respectively), and they often coexist in the same love relationship.

Completely selfless love can be self-defeating. One who places the desires and comforts of his lover above his own, in total fashion, may be pathologically insecure, and he will deprive his lover of a major source of reward, that is, the ability to please him in turn.

Today, there has been a movement among many young people urging an all-embracing love for mankind. While there is much to be said for this, the abstract love for humanity is a phenomenon of a different order from the specific love for an individual, and they should not be confused.

Women's liberation movements may come to influence child rearing practices and, hence, our early love experiences. A change in later attitudes must follow. If men and women approach each other more closely in attitudes and interests, love between them could be enhanced. How much influence on love these movements will really exert remains to be seen.

164

There are far more intricacies to love than we can possibly discuss in this book. Our main goal has been to describe the major principles governing love relationships, and to illustrate them sufficiently to allow the reader a better understanding of his own loves and those of others. Many questions have gone unanswered, of course. In this final chapter, we shall choose a few additional issues to discuss, primarily to illustrate again how an understanding of love within the framework of learning theory can be applied to a question about interpersonal relations. In addition, as a nod toward recognizing the fast-changing character of our world, we shall spend the final sections of this book looking at some current trends and possible future developments.

## Broken Hearts

In Chapter X, we discussed loss of love as a kind of mutual collapse of the relationship, leading to divorce or separation. But it is, of course, not always the case that the loss of love is suffered equally by both partners. One may die, or more commonly, one may want out; the other may not. And one is then left as mourner—still in love. What does it take to mend a broken heart? Is time, alone, sufficient to heal the hurt? Or must other events take place before we recover from a lost love? In trying to answer these questions, we must again consider how extinction or unlearning takes place. In the instance of mourning for a lost love, the issue becomes a bit complicated.

We have adopted the view that love is strong approach behavior—approach to a lover who has reinforced us in many, in varied, and in unpredictable ways. The sight of our lovers comes to evoke good feeling, hope, or the pleasurable anticipation of a rewarding interaction. It soon comes about that the mere thought of our lovers (symbolic representation) evokes this same pleasurable anticipation. And, as love grows, scenes, events, experiences, and moods shared with our lovers all take on the capacity to evoke the thought or image of the lover; the pleasurable anticipation follows in turn. This is not to say that we actually come to sense a chain or series of discrete associations with A leading to B leading to C: familiar scene leading to thoughts of the lover leading to pleasurable anticipation. The association is immediate; the experience all of one piece. The familiar scene or event seems to trigger directly the pleasurable expectancy of interacting with our lovers.

In mourning, this anticipatory response is blocked by the compelling realization that the lover is gone. It is very much the frustrative experience we described in Chapter VIII. In mourning, we yearn to do so, but we cannot follow through; and we know that we cannot. A ready analogy comes to mind. Suppose you are really enthusiastic about fried catfish. One evening rather late, reminded of catfish by a magazine illustration, your appetite fully whetted (high anticipation), you call a friend to arrange a late dinner. The friend points out immediately that the one restaurant serving this delicacy is closed at that hour. Although your consequent feeling of frustrated anticipation would be more accurately described as disappointment, it is, in milder form, much the same emotion suffered in mourning a lost love. In both instances, pleasurable anticipation has been blocked.

If a psychologist, possessing total control over the social environment, were called in to engineer the treatment of mourning, he would reverse the learning stages described above. If he could perfectly arrange events, he would see to it that the loved one was physically present on many, many occasions, taking care on each occasion to insure the total absence of reinforcement. With continuing nonreinforcement, love would eventually extinguish. The sight of, and the thought of, the lover would no longer evoke the pleasurable anticipation (now extinguished). And scenes, events, experiences, and moods that formerly triggered pleasurable anticipations of loving interactions would be automatically "neutralized." This describes the fastest and surest route to the extinction of mourning. Unfortunately, it also describes an impossible solution; clearly one not adaptable to the mourning widow or the recipient of a "Dear John" letter, for, in both cases, the lover is unavailable for direct extinction. What then is the solution to this one-way loss of love? It is indirect; hence slower.

When we lose a loved one and, therefore, cannot directly extinguish love, we can extinguish mourning only by redirecting the associations that evoke thoughts of the lover. The scenes, events, experiences, and moods that remind us of our lovers must be established as cues to other thoughts. To accomplish this, we must experience the situations that evoke the old anticipatory responses. The least effective way of getting over a lost love is to mourn passively. To weaken the expectation of doing rewarding things with a particular someone, we must do these things without him. Associations of scenes and events with thoughts of the lover will give way slowly to associations with other thoughts.

This does not mean that we should undertake a frenzied and false new existence the moment we lose a lover. This could be self-defeating, since behavior that is totally forced is more likely to be punishing than rewarding. But it does mean that, as soon as we are able, we should make a start at sampling the activities we formerly enjoyed with our lovers. In addition, we should undertake novel, exploratory activities around which we can build entirely new sets of pleasurable expectations.

When a well-meaning friend tries to cheer up his broken-hearted buddy by urging varied entertainment, he is operating on a sound principle. We would only caution him to keep the pressure weak to allow some time for the immediate mourning responses to wear off a bit; not to force unwelcome activity on an overly reluctant friend. New experience, not time alone, then, is the mender of broken hearts.

It is interesting to note here a major distinction between liking a person and loving him (Rubin, 1970). If we lose someone we like, we miss him but we do not mourn his loss. We have come to like and admire him because of qualities we value and reinforcements we have received, but we have not developed this general, nonspecific expectation of pleasure that creates love. Hence our missing him is more circumscribed and limited; easier to extinguish.

## Love and Hate

In this book, we have rarely mentioned hate. And yet our folklore abounds with beliefs about the close relationship between love and hate. What is hate? What relationship does it bear to love? These are not empty questions and they invite answers. We shall try to give them, but first we must define hate.

One predominant form of hate involves responses quite the opposite of love. We wish to avoid the hated person. We are uncomfortable when he is around; expecting some unpleasant consequence of his presence. We perceive him as threatening. If we are honest about hate, we wish ill of the hated person; we would find at least some measure of satisfaction in his destruction. Anxiety, avoidance, and malevolence; are these not, indeed, the opposite responses to those we have called love? Yes, they are. So where is the connection between love and hate, hinted at in philosophy, poetry, song, and saying?

To answer this, we must examine the conditions necessary to produce this kind of hate. What we have described as hate is clearly a learned set of reactions to a stimulus that has taken on strongly aversive or punishing characteristics. Just as in love, these are general in nature. If we are punished by someone in a predictable fashion under only limited circumstances, we may learn to fear that person or simply to avoid him, but only under the particular circumstances that signal punishment. However, this it not hate. This is dislike, or even fear. Hate, as love, is a broad and deep response. If we enjoy the company of an admired person only at specified or particular times, we would be said to like, not love, him. And so it goes with disliking. It is specific. Love and hate, on the other hand, are general and herein lies a measure of their similarity.

The development of hatred requires, as does love, extensive interaction with the hated person. It is reasonable to ask why someone would continue to interact with another person who has so often led to punishment. Why would anyone maintain that relationship long enough for true hate to develop? The answer to this question lies partly in the structure of families, and partly in the complexity of human relationships. A young child cannot readily escape an unpredictably cruel and punitive father. Children are often reared by, or with, those not of their choosing. Many marriages, long turned sour, are held together by religious or other considerations apart from the true desires of the couple. So we can be placed by circumstances in situations which, by choice, we would avoid. And hatred, thus, can grow as we are forced into contact with someone who is either intentionally or unintentionally punishing.

Moreover, strange as it may sound, we may actually live by choice with someone we hate. The complexity of human affairs is such that we often maintain conflicting relationships with the same person. All of us are capable of being both rewarding and punishing to others, and in our most intimate relationships we often are. The clear implication of this is that we may love and hate the same person. Psychologists call this ambivalence, and it is not uncommon. There is no logical reason why we should not learn that the same person can give us both pleasure and pain. When this happens, our consequent approach and escape responses do not merely cancel out; they may coexist in the form of conflict (Chapter VIII). The result is usually, that at any given moment, one of these responses predominates and the other is temporarily inactive. In fact, since we normally attempt to avoid unpleasant experiences and emotions, we usually make effort to express love and approach responses to people about whom we are in reality quite ambivalent. Hate, being an unpleasant and socially less acceptable response, is generally the emotion that goes unexpressed overtly. Sometime, when we inhibit the feeling of hate almost totally, psychologists say that we are "repressing" this emotion. It is not wiped out, however, even when we repress it. It makes its presence felt. We experience vague tension and we may express aggressive behavior toward the hated person in indirect or subtle ways that we do not even recognize as destructive.

Other ways in which the hate side of our ambivalent feelings manifests itself can sometimes be rather direct. Violent arguments with spouses or family members in which we "say things we don't really mean" primarily to hurt that person are released expressions of hate in an explosive form.

Some ambivalence is present in almost every close human relationship. It is a rare (possibly nonexistent) human being who consistently and exclusively rewards anyone.

It is often the case that our efforts to deny anger, or negative feelings in general, lead to more trouble than the anger itself. Desperate denial of angry feelings can be more disruptive than expressing them. And small annoyances can grow into great hatred if we continue this.

Love and hate, then, are related in two ways. Conceptually, they are both strong responses to generalized, secondary reinforcers; love, an approach to a positive signal; and hate, an avoidance response to a threatening one. In addition, they often coexist in the same human relationship, in varying degree.

### The "You Always Come Before Me" love

Romantics insist that the epitome of love is found in the conviction that the loved person's welfare and happiness must always come before our own; in other words, in a selfless love that allows us to be happy only when our lovers are. We have indicated earlier, that loving usually involves pleasure in "giving." We have emphasized that lovers strongly value and are moved to protect each other. Does it follow then, that the stronger these feelings, the truer the love? The answer is "no." The motivation behind these "unselfish" feelings comes from several related sources. For example: we obviously wish to protect and retain that which gives us pleasure; we usually find that reward from our lovers is greater when they are happy; we are pleased and reassured about ourselves when we are able to bring joy to someone of value to us; and the happier we can make our lovers, the more likely it is that they will wish to stay with and reward us. It is these last two sources of motivation that can become pathologically strong, often creating painful conflict in both parties.

It has been repeatedly stressed that virtually all of us suffer from some degree of inferiority and insecurity feeling. And so, we usually respond positively to any evidence of our worth and value to other people. We are motivated, then, to make our loved ones happy because, for one thing, their happiness demonstrates our value. But, once again, we run into problems when our views of ourselves are pathologically low. This can express itself in an insatiable drive to prove to ourselves that we are really capable of pleasing someone else and of keeping him happy. If, as a consequence, we subordinate our own pleasure fully, we establish the paradoxical position of depriving our loved ones of an important factor in their contentment: *their* ability to make *us* happy.

An even more damaging situation can arise as a consequence of extreme insecurity feeling. Fear of loss of a loved one can lead to frantic attempts to make him happy. And again, trying too hard not only makes us uncomfortable but can also be self-defeating; our anxiety injects disruptive tension into the relationship.

Giving, and especially giving happiness to the other, is surely a beautiful and essential part of a warm love relationship. Couples who experience their feelings in either a weak form or not at all, are obviously handicapped in their loving. The all-demanding, all-receiving love of infancy has little place in adulthood. But it is also true that at the other extreme, the dedicated giver, who subordinates himself completely to his lover's wishes is likely to lose not only himself but the entire relationship as well.

### Directions

Up to this point, most of what we have said about love would have almost equal application 20, 30, or even 50 years ago. While not denying that some changes in the expression of love (and particularly in the expression of sex) have taken place in the last few decades, we have argued that most of these are shallow and that true freedom in matters of the heart, sexual or otherwise, is neither here yet nor an immediate prospect. The principles we have developed are intended to apply across the cultural changes that are taking place around us at an accelerating pace. Some of these changes, however, actually involve love and sex directly and may influence their essential character in the future. Obviously, we can only speculate as to how.

The generation born after World War II offered love to offset the dehumanizing materialism of our culture. The offer, for the most part, was refused by a society that seemed to feel only mild sympathy or total revulsion. But some influence has been felt. First phrases, then feelings, have crept into our social relationships. While the late 1960s seemed to bring some disillusionment, many of love's advocates still cling to their conceptions of a brave new world, and the rest of the country has begun, at least, to let its hair down a little bit.

We are not yet able to assess completely what influence today's love culture will have on the rest of our society. It is not even entirely clear what kind of love was (and is) being espoused. Many people believe that the entire idea was free sexual love. Some believe that it was an all-accepting love of humanity. It is apparent that both of these elements exist in the movement; and often, the former is given as a logical consequence of the latter. The idea of free love does not seem to have seduced many of us; and the acceptance and love of all people has obviously not become the rule. But discussion and freer acceptance of the love concept are probably slowly leading to an attitude change. What can we expect, or perhaps hope for?

We have seen that love of humanity is a highly abstract type of response (Chapter XI). It is a consequence of generalization from early experiences with people. It cannot be established by edict. We cannot say, "love all humanity" and expect it to occur. A much longer learning process is required. Moreover, loving all of humanity is a response of a different order from that of loving a specific human being. "I love all people, therefore, I love you," may sound perfectly logical but it involves the use of the verb, love, in somewhat different ways. Love for a specific person is an experience that involves learning to discriminate that person from all other people. We prefer his company to that of others. Since some people are more rewarding to us than others, we shall continue (whatever our level of love for humanity), to form specific love attachments. We can surely love people in general, and, in a more specific sense, love several people at the same time. But we should never expect to love all people as individuals.

On the other hand, even if we cannot suddenly love humanity as a whole, or everyone individually, perhaps the intellectual acceptance of the idea can lead to social benefit. We may learn that if we are pleasant and supportive of others, that they will be pleasant and rewarding in return, instead of rejecting us (as we seem to often fear). With enough experience this could become widespread and eventually make loving humanity a more widely adopted attitude. Whether it leads to more love of any sort, or merely greater social reward, it surely seems a desirable change.

## Women's Liberation

Another recent trend that carries considerable potential to influence our love lives is the movement toward a redefinition of the woman's role in our society. The past few years have witnessed the development of women's liberation organizations, all dedicated, in one way or another, to broadening the role of the woman. The movement, in general, has progressed from the butt of jokes to impetus for congressional action. Today, women possess a legislated right to much of what was, previously, exclusively a man's world.

In their relationship with men, women have sought to move from status symbol to status seeker, and from sex object to sex partner. They have lobbied for equality in bed and business, and for freedom from being assigned the restricted roles of babysitter and housewife. If, in fact, the traditional difference in sex roles becomes obliterated, or even seriously weakened, then the effects on our love relationships will truly prove to be far-reaching. The family constellation that has served as the basis for early love development will obviously change drastically as a consequence. The all-providing mother will no longer serve as the object of first love. But this, as we shall see, is not necessarily bad.

The traditional relationships in marriage (Chapter IX) would undergo immense change. There is evidence that this change is already taking place throughout industrialized Western cultures. The balance of power within the family is influenced by a wife's extended role outside the family (particularly in lower class families). With the husband no longer the sole provider and major source of interaction with the outside world, he is also no longer quite so dominant within the family structure (Haavio-Mannila, 1969). In some ways, this may also be for the better. One of the greatest handicaps faced in marriage resides in the fact that husbands and wives, because of clearly differing sex roles, share too few values and too few interests. Perhaps similar societal roles would tend to close this gap.

There are many unanswered questions, of course. For example what will replace present child-rearing practices? This issue has been addressed by some of the woman's organizations themselves. The care of children could be, they say, at least partly provided for by the state in the form of child care centers. And, the father could share the task to a much greater extent than he does currently.

Some knowledge exists concerning the effects on children of rearing by professional groups (other than custodial orphanages), in a manner quite similar to the methods currently proposed. Children reared in Israeli Kibbutzim have been studied extensively (Spiro, 1958) and found to be well adjusted on the whole, intensely loyal to their group, not especially oriented toward their families of biological origin, and fully capable of forming good love relationships. There may be some advantage in having more than one loving and warm mother figure during infancy. The child is clearly not so fully at the mercy of one, possibly idiosyncratic, set of parents who, exclusively, define love and man-woman relationships for him.

A second question presents itself; one that is more difficult to answer. Can women's interests and pursuits really approximate those of men, or are there biologically determined ("natural") differences? In Chapter XII, we discussed the effects of hormones (male and female) on the interests and behavior of humans. It is apparent that sex hormones do direct, or at least influence, types of activity and the interests of the individual. However, we also saw that many of the differences between men and women in the interests they hold are due to learning (socialization experiences). These, of course, are modifiable. And to that extent, man and woman could be brought somewhat closer together in their roles. It remains to be seen how much of this will actually take place, and what effect it will have.

## Love

Love is a natural human response that will take place under the proper learning conditions. The world may change, technologically, politically, socially and in other ways, but we shall continue to love the people who reward us in many and varied ways although the kinds of behaviors that are important and reinforcing to us may change. The expression and the rituals of love may also change. But love, itself, will continue as a basic psychological phenomenon.

We have tried to explain and illustrate the principles of love. And we have selectively addressed some specific questions of how love manifests itself in today's Western culture. The book is intended to be suggestive, not exhaustive. We hope the reader will find it possible to apply the framework to discover answers to specific personal questions he may have. The ultimate test of theory is always its applicability. Most certainly, we hope that we have added a bit to the reader's ability to enjoy interpersonal relationships.

# References

Akpaffiong, J. Personal communication, Atlanta University, 1970.

Aronson, E., & Linder, D. Gain and loss of esteem as determinants of interpersonal attractiveness. *Journal of Experimental Social Psychology*, 1965, 1, 156–171.

Barry, W. A. Marriage research and conflict: an integrative review. *Psychological Bulletin*, 1970, 73, 41–54.

Blood, R. O., & Wolfe, D. M. *Husbands and wives: the dynamics of married living.* New York: Free Press, 1960.

Brown, D. G. Sex-role development in a changing culture. *Psychological Bulletin*, 1958, 55, 232–242.

Caprio, F. S. *The sexually adequate female.* New York: Citadel Press, 1953.

Christensen, H. T. Children in the family: relationship of number and spacing to marital success. *Journal of Marriage and Family*, 1968, 30, 283–289.

Cox, F. D. *Youth, marriage, and the seductive society.* (Rev. ed.), Dubuque, Iowa: W. C. Brown, 1968.

Dobzhansky, T. *Mankind evolving,* New Haven: Yale University Press, 1962.

Dollard, J., & Miller, N. E. *Personality and psychotherapy.* New York: McGraw-Hill, 1950.

Eibl-Ebesfeldt, I. *Ethology: the biology of behavior.* New York: Holt, Rinehart, & Winston, 1970, Chapters 5 and 6.

Ellis, A. *Sex without guilt.* New York: Lyle Stuart, 1958.

Faber, N. G. Sex for credit. *Look Magazine*, April 1, 1969, 33, No. 7, 39–45.

Festinger, L. *A theory of cognitive dissonance.* Evanston, Ill.: Row, Peterson, 1957.

Ford, C., & Beach, F. A. *Patterns of sexual behavior.* New York: Harper & Brothers, Publishers and Paul B. Hoeber, Medical Books, 1951.

Freud, S. *New introductory lectures on psychoanalysis.* New York: W. W. Norton, 1933.

Fromm, E. *The art of loving.* New York: Harper and Row, 1956.

Glick, P. C. *American families.* New York: Wiley, 1957.

Grunt, J., & Young, W. Psychological modification of fatigue following orgasm (ejaculation) in the male guinea pig. *Journal of Comparative and Physiological Psychology*, 1952, 45, 508–510.

Haavio-Mannila, E. Some consequences of women's emancipation. *Journal of Marriage and the Family*, 1969, 31, 128–144.

Hettlinger, R. F. *Living with sex, the student's dilemma.* New York: Seabury Press, 1966.

Kallman, F. J. Twins and susceptibility to overt male homosexuality. *American Journal of Human Genetics,* 1952, 4, 136–146.

Kallman, F. J. *Heredity in health and mental disorder.* New York: Norton, 1953.

Karlen, A. The sexual revolution is a myth. In J. G. Roloff (Ed.) *Encounter.* Beverly Hills, Calif.: Glencoe Press, 1970.

Katz, D. *Gestalt psychology.* New York: Ronald Press, 1950.

Kinsey, A. C., Pomeroy, W. B., & Martin, C. E. *Sexual behavior in the human male.* Philadelphia: W. B. Saunders, 1948.

Kinsey, W. H., Pomeroy, W. B., Martin, C. E., & Gebhard, P. H. *Sexual behavior in the human female.* Philadelphia: W. B. Saunders, 1953.

Kolodny, R. C., Masters, W. H., Hendryx, J., & Toro, S. Plasma testosterone and semen analysis in male homosexuals. *New England Journal of Medicine,* 1971, 285, 1170–1174.

Kronhausen, P., & Kronhausen, E. *Sex histories of American college men.* New York: Ballantine Books, 1960.

Kronhausen, P., & Kronhausen, E. *The sexually responsive woman.* New York: Ballantine Books, 1964.

Landis, P. H. Making the most of marriage. New York: Appleton-Century-Crofts, 1970.

Landis, C., Landis, A. T., Boles, M. M., Metzger, H. F., Petts, M. W., D'Esopo, D. A., Moloy, H. C., Klugman, S. J., & Dickinson, R. L. *Sex in development.* New York: Paul B. Hoeber, 1940.

Langdon, G., & Stout, I. *These well adjusted children.* New York: John Day, 1951.

Lively, E. I., Toward concept clarification: the case of marital interaction. *Journal of Marriage and Family,* 1969, 31, 108–114.

Lowen, A. *Love and orgasm.* New York: New American Library, 1965.

Luckey, E. B., & Nass, G. D. A comparison of sexual attitudes and behavior in an international sample. *Journal of Marriage and Family,* 1969, 31, 364–369.

Masters, W. H., & Johnson, V. E. The human female: anatomy of sexual response. *Minnesota Medicine,* 1960, 43, 31–36.

Masters, W. H., & Johnson, V. E. *Human sexual response.* Boston: Little, Brown, 1966.

Masters, W. H., & Johnson, V. E. *Human sexual inadequacy.* Boston: Little, Brown, 1970.

May, R. *Love and will.* New York: W. W. Norton, 1970.

Miller, H., & Rivenbark, W. H. Sexual differences in physical attractiveness as a determinant of heterosexual liking. *Psychological Reports,* 1970, 27, 701–702.

Miller, H., & Wilson, W. Relation of sexual behaviors, values, and conflict of avowed happiness and personal adjustment. *Psychological Reports,* 1968, 23, 1075–1086.

Money, J. Sexual dimorphism and homosexual gender identity. *Psychological Bulletin,* 1970, 74, 425–440.

Mowrer, O. H. *Learning theory and behavior.* New York: Wiley, 1960.

Pfeil, E. Expectations when entering into marriage. *Journal of Marriage and Family*, 1965, **30**, 161–165.

Reich, W. *The function of the orgasm.* New York: Orgone Institute Press, 1942.

Rubin, Z. The measurement of romantic love. Paper read at American Psychological Association, Miami Beach, Florida, 1970.

Rubin, Z. The measurement of romantic love. *Journal of Personality and Social Psychology*, 1970b, September, 16, 265–273.

Rutledge, A. L. *Pre-marital counseling.* Cambridge, Mass.: Schenkman Publishing, 1966.

Scanzoni, J. A social system analysis of dissolved and existing marriages. *Journal of Marriage and Family*, 1968, 30, 452–461.

Sheffield, F. D., Wulff, J. J., & Baker, R. Reward value of copulation without sex-drive reduction. *Journal of Comparative and Physiological Psychology*, 1951, **44**, 3–8.

Siegel, P. S., & Pilgrim, F. The effect of monotony on the acceptance of food. *American Journal of Psychology*, 1958, 71, 756–759.

Spiro, M. E. *Children of the kibbutz.* Cambridge, Mass.: Harvard University Press, 1958.

Stalling, R. B. Personality similarity and evaluative meaning as conditioners of attraction. *Journal of Personal and Social Psychology*, 1970, **14**, 77–82.

Sullivan, H. S. *The interpersonal theory of psychiatry.* New York: Norton, 1953.

Tenenbaum, S. *A psychologist looks at marriage.* Cranberry, New Jersey: A. S. Barnes, 1968.

Thomas, M. M. Children with absent fathers. *Journal of Marriage and Family*, 1968, 30, 89–96.

Trainer, R. *The male homosexual today.* New York: Macfadden-Bartell, 1970.

United States Department of Health Education and Welfare Monthly Vital Statistics Report Provisional Statistics. Annual Summary for the United States, 1969, Births, Deaths, and Divorces, Vol. 18, No. 13, Oct. 21, 1970.

Wainwright, L. Another sort of love story. *Life Magazine*, January 22, 1971, 70, No. 2, 2B.

Walster, E. Self-esteem and romantic attraction. Paper read at American Psychological Association, Miami Beach, Florida, 1970.

Walster, E., Aronson, V., Abraham, D., & Rottman, L. Importance of physical attractiveness in dating behavior. *Journal of Personality and Social Psychology*, 1966, **4**, 508–516.

Walster, E., & Bersheid, E. Adrenaline makes the heart grow fonder. *Psychology Today*, June 1971, **5**, No. 1.

Wilson, W. R. Relation of sexual behaviors, values, and conflicts to avowed happiness. *Psychological Reports*, 1965, **17**, 371–378.

Zuckerman, M. Physiological measures of sexual arousal in the human. *Psychological Bulletin*, 1971, **75**, 297–329.

# INDEX

179